LEARN BLACK AMERICAN SIGN LANGUAGE

LEARN BLACK AMERICAN SIGN LANGUAGE

A HISTORY AND COMPLETE BEGINNER'S GUIDE WITH OVER 200 WORDS AND PHRASES

FRANKLIN R. JONES JR.

wellfleet
press

CONTENTS

Preserving Language and Legacy

What is Black American Sign Language (BASL)? How do—and should—we define this term?

BASL is the variety of American Sign Language (ASL) that developed in the segregated schools for Deaf African American children in the pre–Civil Rights era. It shows differences from the ASL used by most white signers in lexicon, phonology, syntax, and discourse (see page 9).

In some respects, BASL is a conservative dialect. Specifically, several phonological features are more likely to be realized in the standard (or citation) form taught in ASL classes and used in ASL dictionaries than is the case in most white varieties of ASL.

THE NOBLEST GIFT

As I look back on my life, I am grateful for how I learned sign language. I lost my hearing at the age of five and struggled with the English language. I attended a "regular" public school (that is, a school for hearing students) from the first to seventh grades and spoke African American English (AAE) in my home and community. I learned sign language at the age of twelve. I struggled with my identities as a Black Deaf young girl. Identity exploration is a natural part of adolescence, but because of that, it's also a time of confusion.

After a frustrating experience in public school, I transferred to the segregated Alabama School for the Negro Deaf and Blind. Unbeknownst to me was BASL in its originality. At my new school, I found a sense of belonging within the community and embraced Black Deaf culture and language. I learned the language by following along with my fellow students. Later, I graduated from the integrated Alabama School for the Deaf and Gallaudet University.

Fast-forward to my entering Gallaudet University's Administrative and Supervision PhD program. It was when the fullness of my experience with BASL hit me. I contemplated George Veditz's quotation: "[Sign language is] the noblest gift God has given to Deaf people." I also contemplated

The South Carolina Institution for the Education of the Deaf and Dumb and the Blind was founded in 1849, featuring a Colored Department that would not be integrated until 1967.

a quote I had come across in Ernest Hairston and Linwood Smith's 1983 book *Black and Deaf in America*: that there is a "Black way of signing used by Black deaf people in their own cultural milieu—among families and friends, in social gatherings, and in deaf clubs." I felt it was a ripe time to analyze the Black Sign Language that I had learned as a teenager in Alabama.

THE BLACK ASL PROJECT

In 2005, I became involved with the Black ASL Project when linguist Dr. Ceil Lucas and I met one day after I successfully defended my dissertation, "The Education of Black Deaf Americans in the 20th Century: Policies and Implications for Administrators in Deaf Schools," which covers the experiences of former students, faculty, and staff at segregated schools for the Deaf in the South. Dr. Lucas was at my dissertation defense and proposed an idea that we should work together to do a research project on a sign language variety used at the segregated schools.

This was a golden opportunity, but it was a difficult beginning. Twice we applied to the National Science Foundation (NSF) and twice we were rejected. But, on our third try, we succeeded in obtaining the necessary funding from NSF to carry out our project. As the adage says, "If at first you do not succeed, try, try again."

Defining Moments

We traveled to six states to interview participants for our project. It felt surreal because I attended both the Alabama School for the Negro Deaf and the Alabama School for the Deaf in Talladega, Alabama, United States, so I could identify with the stories from the former students we interviewed. I thought about the time when I was a student: how I had struggled to obtain a better education and struggled to understand why I wasn't grasping the ASL taught at the white Deaf school. The Black ASL Project gave me an opportunity to tell stories about the Black Deaf experience from our perspective and in our language.

The impact of the Black ASL Project was so much greater than I expected. I never dreamed of the impact it would have on the Deaf community, the Black Deaf community, and the interpreting field. It was wonderful to collaborate and work with my three coauthors (Dr. Ceil Lucas, Dr. Robert Bayley, and Dr. Joseph Hill) and our research assistants. I felt honored to be able to tell the stories of the project's participants through our research and give them a voice. We validated their school experiences.

Creating Inclusive Communication

The Black ASL Project consists of groundbreaking research and created the Black ASL Mosaic which analyzed eight different linguistic features that defined BASL as a distinct variety of ASL.

Black ASL Mosaic

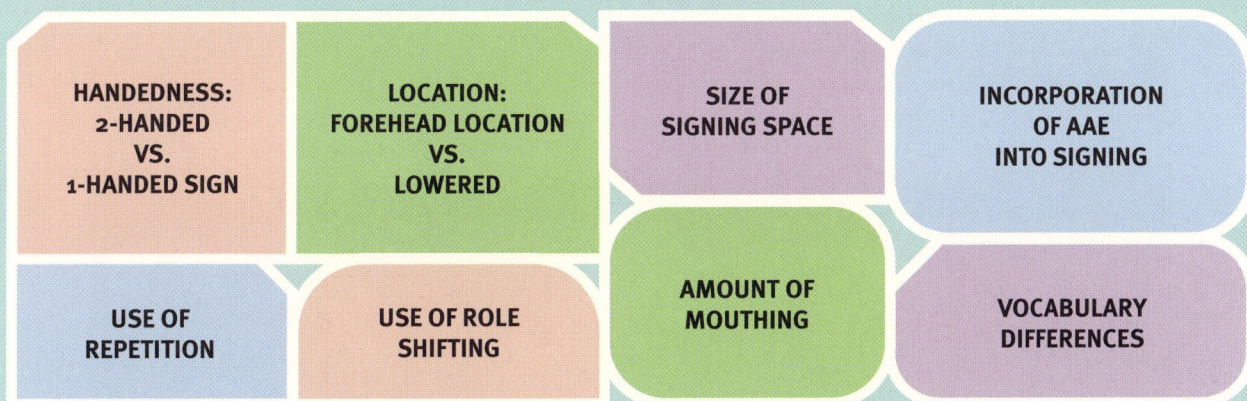

| HANDEDNESS: 2-HANDED VS. 1-HANDED SIGN | LOCATION: FOREHEAD LOCATION VS. LOWERED | SIZE OF SIGNING SPACE | INCORPORATION OF AAE INTO SIGNING |
| USE OF REPETITION | USE OF ROLE SHIFTING | AMOUNT OF MOUTHING | VOCABULARY DIFFERENCES |

TWO-HANDED VERSUS ONE-HANDED SIGNS

In ASL, there are words that are signed with two hands or one hand. Additionally, two-handed signs can usually be signed with one hand instead. The Black ASL Project revealed that Black signers more consistently use two-handed signs than white signers.

LOCATION: FOREHEAD VERSUS LOWERED

In ASL, there are several words that can be signed at the forehead level or lower. For example, the word "know" is usually signed above the eyebrows. The Black ASL Project found that BASL signs the word "know" at the forehead level, or even at the middle of the forehead. These are thought to be older versions of this sign (see page 14 for more details).

SIZE OF THE SIGNING SPACE

The signing "space" refers to how much space the average individual takes up with their hands when using ASL. BASL signers use a larger signing space than those using ASL.

INCORPORATION OF AAE INTO SIGNING

Contact with African American English resulted in higher instances of AAE being incorporated into the vocabulary of Black signers. AAE can be incorporated in several different ways:
1. Spoken and signed (called code-mixing)
2. Signed in BASL (called borrowing)
3. Spoken and not signed
(called code-switching, see page 15)

REPETITION

The Black ASL Project also found that BASL signers use more clausal or phrasal repetition compared to ASL. Repetition can be used to emphasize a point, like signing "HAVE SON, HAVE SON NOW" to express the idea "I have a son now."

ROLE SHIFTING

In ASL, role shifting refers to what in English is called indirect speech. Individuals report what others have said (what is called constructed dialogue) and take on the role of the other individual in the interaction they are reporting (constructed action). The research carried out by the Black ASL Project found that Black signers are more likely to use both constructed dialogue and constructed action than white signers.

MOUTHING

Mouthing refers to mouthing the English words along with the words you are signing in ASL. The Black ASL Project reported that Black signers used very little to no mouthing at all compared to white signers.

VOCABULARY DIFFERENCES

Throughout the interviews conducted by the team working on the Black ASL Project, Black signers often brought up that they used different signs for common words like "movie" or "color" compared to ASL.

African American schoolchildren posed outside a segregated one-room schoolhouse in South Carolina, 1905.

Multigenerational Black Deaf Families

During the interviews, we also found that there were approximately nine individuals from several generations of Black Deaf families, which ran against the general belief at the time that such families were rare. Since I have two Deaf sisters and a Deaf first cousin in my family and my colleague and coauthor Dr. Joseph Hill is also from a Black Deaf family, this finding was important to me.

In the years following the conclusion of the Black ASL Project, we began another project on Black Deaf families with the interviewees from the Black ASL Project at the National Black Deaf Advocates Conference in New Orleans, Louisiana, in August 2013 and a few more individuals in Washington, DC in the years after that. It is rewarding for us to meet more Black Deaf individuals who have family members who are also Deaf. The highlight is one family I met where the person I spoke to is the oldest of thirteen siblings and her granddaughter is a fifth-generation member of this Black Deaf family.

The validation of the Black ASL Project and the book we published about it, called *The Hidden Treasure of Black ASL: Its History and Structure*, gave the Black Deaf community a sense of purpose and an opportunity to value their rich history, community, culture, and language. But the Black ASL Project only scratched the surface. There is still so much more work to be done in terms of research on BASL.

LOOKING FORWARD

Research on BASL has increased in the years since the Black ASL Project and only continues to grow. An increase in research is also an increase in interest from the general public about this fascinating, yet less well-known American dialect.

SIGNING BLACK IN AMERICA premiered on television in 2020 and is the first documentary about BASL. BASL today conveys an identity and sense of belonging that mirror spoken language varieties of the African American hearing communities. Different uses of space, hand use, directional movement, and facial expressions are ways that BASL distinguishes itself as a vibrant dialect of ASL. The African American Deaf community is now embracing their unique variety as a symbol of solidarity and a vital part of their identity.

My hope is that this book continues the original ideals and goals of the Black ASL Project and encourages people to learn more about this fascinating dialect and how we can all work together to preserve it for future generations.

Dr. Carolyn McCaskill *is a graduate of the Alabama School for the Deaf and has a BA in psychology with a minor in social work, and an MA in Counseling of the Deaf from Gallaudet University. She received her doctorate in administration and supervision and was the second Black Deaf female to do so from Gallaudet University. She is currently a professor in the ASL & Deaf Studies Department at Gallaudet University and has been teaching since 1996.*

McCaskill is the coauthor of the book and DVD The Hidden Treasure of Black ASL: Its History and Structure. *Carolyn has hosted numerous workshops and seminars related to various aspects of BASL history, community, and culture on a local, national, and global level.*

The History of Black American Sign Language

Black American Sign Language is not a language, but American Sign Language is a language. For many years, the Black Deaf community, or education in general, did not discuss BASL within the Black Deaf community and the Deaf community. By and large, many hidden histories about our Black Deaf history are unknown. One piece of hidden history has been uncovered due to the efforts of Dr. Carolyn McCaskill and her research team, who interviewed Black Deaf people in several states to gather their stories about BASL and reveal what BASL is: a dialect of American Sign Language used by Black Deaf individuals.

How did this dialect develop and why? Is it still used today? To answer these questions, let's go over the history of Black American Sign Language.

BEFORE DESEGREGATION

By the time the Civil War (1861 to 1865) ended in the United States, there was no longer slavery, and all Black people were freed. Black people lived in America's dream and could do what they wanted, like white people. At least, that was the idea.

In reality, discriminatory laws and practices remained in place long after slavery was outlawed in the United States. In the American South, these were called Jim Crow laws, and they were not completely abolished until the Civil Rights Act of 1964 and the Voting Rights Act of 1965. Racial segregation—that is, the separation of people based on their race—was both formally and informally enforced, and schools were no exception. Both Black and white students were required to be segregated in school. They could not see each other or be near each other: They had to attend separate schools entirely.

What about Black Deaf people? Did they receive a formal education like Black hearing people?

Absolutely! Segregation did not impact Black hearing people alone; it also impacted Black Deaf people. Black Deaf students were unschooled for several years until 1869 when the North Carolina School for the Colored Deaf was established to provide Black Deaf students with an education. Within a few years, other states founded Black Deaf schools to educate Black Deaf children.

What Is Oralism?

In the post–Civil War era, different ideas began to emerge about the best way for Deaf individuals to communicate. Oralism was one of these ideas. People who supported oralism (including Alexander Graham Bell, the inventor of the telephone) believed that Deaf people should not learn sign language because it isolated Deaf people, making them "too different" from hearing people. Instead, Deaf people should only communicate using lipreading and speech. This idea caught on in the late nineteenth century and continued into the early twentieth century.

During the oralist era, Deaf students, both Black and white, were banned from using sign language in school. But oralism transpired differently among Black Deaf students compared to white Deaf students, as the education system was mainly focused on white Deaf individuals while neglecting Black Deaf students. Although Black Deaf students received an education in school, they were not indoctrinated to learn how to speak like white Deaf students were. White Deaf students were required to learn how to speak and they were also expected to be "normal" like hearing people in school. Additionally, they were not allowed to learn sign language in class or they would be punished for using it.

Black Deaf students did not have the same experience. They were not forced to learn how to speak in school but used their authentic BASL. For decades, they continued using their BASL as their primary language and were able to preserve sign language during the height of the oralist movement.

At the time of segregation, schools in thirteen states in the South were segregated: Alabama, Arkansas, Florida, Georgia, Kentucky, Louisiana, Mississippi, North Carolina, Oklahoma, South Carolina, Tennessee, Texas, and Virginia. Like with Black and white hearing students, Black and white Deaf students could not be present in the same classroom, or even be in the same building. There were two different types of schools for segregation: It could have been two distinct campuses in various locations where the students would never see each other, or a building on campus called a "department" that was an isolated building on the campus for Black Deaf students only. Because of this geographical and social isolation, Black Deaf students birthed Black American Sign Language so they could communicate with each other.

Where did these signs come from? Most Black Deaf individuals used Home sign systems with their families, or signs that family members used to communicate with each other that didn't have an "official" source or word list. Some of these individuals came from multigenerational families that had their own versions of Black American Sign Language, which they shared with the community. When these individuals enrolled in school, they formed a new BASL with the Black Deaf community that attended the Deaf school, combining their Home sign with those of others from multigenerational families.

Because Black Deaf people lived in different states and regions, and because there was no standardized BASL, it goes without saying that regional variations of BASL also developed. Residents of different states developed a unique sign vocabulary, which differs greatly from ASL and Southern American English. Additionally, the way Black Deaf people use BASL is different, which Dr. Carolyn McCaskill discusses on page 8.

The Significance of Groups

The Black Deaf community learned and preserved BASL through several different means besides the sign language they were taught in school.

Organizations: Black Deaf individuals created their own clubs and organizations because they were segregated from nationwide Deaf groups (such as the National Association of the Deaf, or NAD), and Black groups (such as the National Association for the Advancement of Colored People, or NAACP) did not adequately address their needs. These clubs and organizations for Black Deaf individuals were places where people could freely express themselves and build local communities.

Families: Multigenerational Deaf families would communicate with each other using their own signs. Children using their own sign language with their parents would bring these signs to school, no doubt adding to the linguistic wealth of BASL. However, there is still a lot that we don't know about Black Deaf multigenerational families.

BLACK AMERICAN SIGN LANGUAGE AFTER DESEGREGATION

In 1954, the landmark Supreme Court case Brown v. Board of Education banned segregation in public schools because it violated the Fourteenth Amendment, failing to protect all citizens in the United States and ensuring they received the same treatment under the law. All schools in the South were mandated to desegregate, both Black and white.

However, desegregation did not happen overnight. It took a while to desegregate schools in each state. The Maryland School for the Deaf was the first desegregated school in the South in 1958. Then other schools in other states started desegregating, with Louisiana having the last Deaf school to desegregate in 1978. That was when all Black and white Deaf students integrated and met in school.

At first, Black and white Deaf students could not understand each other; Black Deaf and white teachers could not understand each other. Why? Because their sign languages differed. Black Deaf students felt they were not at the level of white Deaf students and teachers because of BASL and thought they should surrender their BASL. During the time of segregation, the schools Black Deaf students attended had fewer resources and less access to funding than the schools for white students, so as a result, the Black Deaf students felt their education was of a lower quality. They decided to code-switch to match the white Deaf ASL because they felt that ASL was much better, prettier, and smarter than BASL.

What Is Code-Switching?

Code-switching refers to the way individuals may change their way of communicating or behaving based on the social context they are in and whom they are interacting with. For example, the way you speak to and interact with your boss is probably different from how you are around your closest friends. In a linguistics context, code-switching often refers to those who know multiple languages or dialects and switch which one they're using depending on the context, sometimes even mid-sentence.

Black Deaf individuals often code-switched: When they went home or socialized with their community, they used BASL, but whenever they were in a white Deaf community, they would use ASL. Black Deaf people couldn't pick one but had to code-switch for both communities to ensure they could understand each other, and they used ASL to be considered intelligent and "equivalent" to their white Deaf peers.

As a result, over the years Black ASL has become more integrated into the ASL standard. That also means the use of BASL has declined (in linguistics, this phenomenon is called "language attrition") because most BASL users have put aside their BASL and use ASL as their primary language.

That doesn't mean BASL has been forgotten; in recent years there have been more efforts to preserve what we still know of BASL. These efforts will be discussed later on page 182.

HOME SIGN LANGUAGE

I am a fourth-generation Deaf individual. The members of my extended family are sixth-generation Deaf individuals. We were born and raised on Wadmalaw Island, South Carolina, a small island in Charleston County, United States. Within my immediate and extended family, there is a mix of Deaf and hearing individuals. The first two generations of Deaf individuals in my family never received a formal education, and their parents used Home sign (page 18) to communicate with them. What makes my family unique is that these first two Deaf generations, along with their hearing relatives, utilized Black Home sign for communication, allowing them to engage in full conversations without limitations.

When faced with new technology, terminology, or concepts difficult to express through gestures, they would either skip that part, point to something, or create a new gesture before resuming the conversation. Although gestures alone are not considered a language, they represent a visible, structured form of communication created to converse with family members. For instance, individuals would invent new signs based on real-life situations such as "moon," "blanket," "hungry," "bird," and "reading." Some gestures convey clear, concrete meanings, while others represent more abstract ideas that are challenging to indicate visually, often supplemented with English mouthing for clarity.

Typically, Home sign tends to be a limited form of communication because Deaf children often experience linguistic deprivation, either by living with hearing families who do not sign or by being isolated from the Deaf community. In such cases, Deaf children and their hearing parents create new signs to communicate, but these often lack grammatical structure. For example, someone might gesture a single word like "eat."

In my family, the last two Deaf generations code-switch between different forms of communication, including BASL, ASL, and African American Vernacular English (AAVE). However, the third Deaf generation (that is, my parents' generation) is more fluent in Home sign than the fourth, which includes me and my older sister. The third Deaf generation can use complex Home sign language with grammatical structures that include facial expressions similar to ASL. For example, they might sign "HUNGRY YOU" ("Are you hungry?") with raised eyebrows, expecting a yes/no response, demonstrating that their Home sign has developed its own grammatical structure.

My family often uses Home sign with mouthing movements to further clarify meaning. A conversation might go as follows:

Person A: WORK YOU GO WHEN?
("When are you going to work?")

Person B: TOMORROW MORNING 6 GO WORK.
("I'm going to work at 6 a.m. tomorrow.")

Person A: WOW! TOMORROW SO EARLY MORNING, WHY?
("Wow! Why so early tomorrow morning?")

Person B: BOSS TOLD ME TOMORROW WORK LOT.
("My boss told me we have to work a lot tomorrow.")

This exchange illustrates our ability to discuss past, present, and future events without limitations.

However, the use of Home sign in my family has begun to diminish, as many family members are no longer present or no longer use it regularly. We still occasionally employ Home sign when interacting with elderly hearing cousins during holidays or other events. There are also a few of my aunts who use Home signs mixed with ASL. Some of our family's signs, such as the sign for "shrimp" represented by a gesture of cutting off its head with the thumb, have been used for so long that they persist in the last two Deaf generations, who now primarily use BASL.

How to Use This Book

This book takes into account the unique history and development of Black American Sign Language and aims to preserve it for future generations. Note that the words in this book are only a small percentage of BASL. Because of how BASL developed, especially after integration, as of 2025 sometimes there is no way of knowing what words originated with BASL and then were later incorporated into American Sign Language. If you already sign ASL, it's possible some of the words you use were influenced by BASL!

Because of the close connection between BASL and ASL, we will begin our journey with the ASL alphabet as an easy reference. Many of the descriptions of the signs in this book will reference handshapes (see page 19) that derive from the ASL alphabet, and there are signs in the African American Vernacular English chapter (page 167) that utilize fingerspelling (words marked with a hashtag [#]), so feel free to stick a bookmark in this section so you can easily flip back to it when needed.

The words in the remaining chapters have been divided into themes like time and weather (page 29), verbs (page 131), or descriptions (page 149). Some themes have fewer words than others, because it is dependent on which words survived to be included in the historical record.

The words featured will either be BASL or Home sign. Words written in the deep-red color are signs that were widely used and could be considered to be part of what an official BASL word list might look like. When a BASL sign is mentioned, I have noted the state or region they originated from when there are multiple variants for one word (see page 14 for why regional variants developed). Some of these words have been sourced from Dr. Carolyn McCaskill's groundbreaking research on Black American Sign Language.

The words designated with a "HOME" icon and a red tinted background have been sourced from my community. By that, I mean signs where they may have originated with my family, and, through our interactions with the larger Black Deaf community, may have then become the main sign for that word in our region. Or it could've happened the other way around: It's not entirely clear how these signs originated. This reflects how Black Deaf individuals communicated with each other in the years during segregation before the widespread adoption of ASL.

In both instances, I will provide descriptions of how these words should be signed, as well as any other things to note. This book also includes a special feature comparing select words to its American Sign Language equivalent to show how they are different. These words will be designated with an "ASL" icon and a green tinted background and will, for the most part, be placed directly below their BASL or Home sign counterpart. For some words, there might not be much of a difference! Did the sign in BASL come first, or ASL?

● **HOME** = Home Sign
● **ASL** = American Sign Language
BASL = Black American Sign Language

Terminology, Explained

Certain terms commonly used in American Sign Language will be utilized to describe the signs in this book. Key ones are listed here.

Handshape refers to the shapes our hands make in order to communicate in sign language. You may see descriptions refer to a "5-handshape" (when you stretch out your fingers so they show an open palm) or "letter-handshape" (when the word requires a handshape of a particular letter in ASL).

Location is also important in sign language, as where you sign a word can change its meaning.

Neutral space is a term used throughout this book. It indicates the general space around you, usually in front of your body or around your head. This is considered the signer's personal space.

One final piece of information: The signs that require use of only one hand can be performed by the left or right hand as it is dependent on the signer's dominant hand. So now that we've covered all the background information you need to know, let's explore the fascinating world of Black American Sign Language together.

Franklin is signing the letter *F* (page 22) and Stephanie is signing the letter *S* (page 25).

THE
AMERICAN
SIGN
LANGUAGE
ALPHABET

A

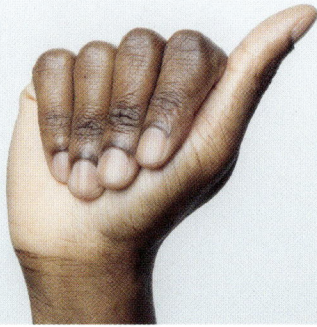

B

C

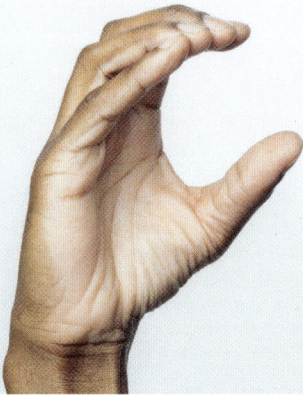

D

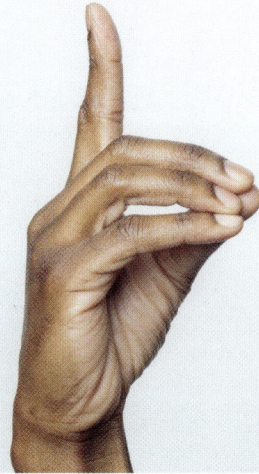

E

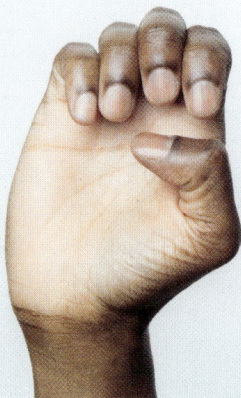

F

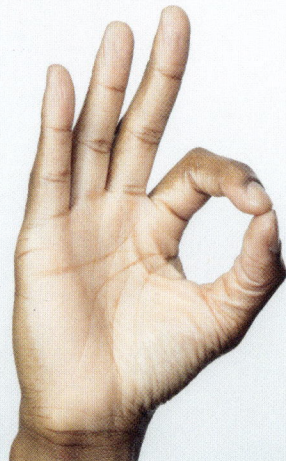

G

H

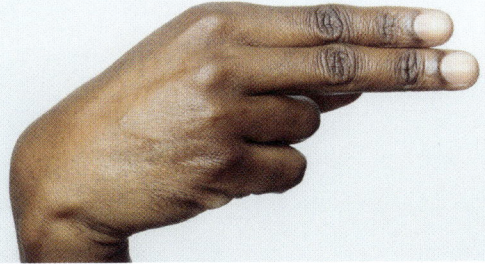

I

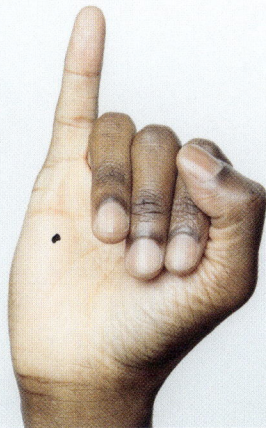

J1

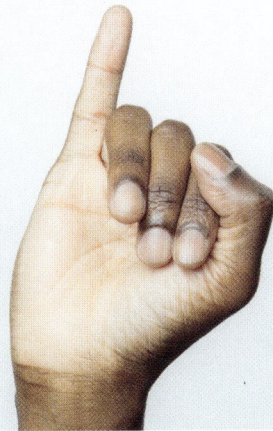

J2

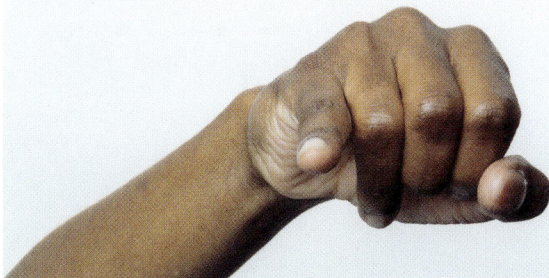

J3

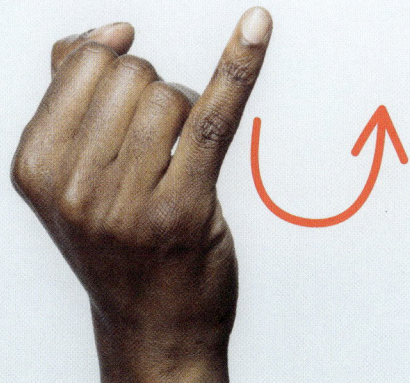

K

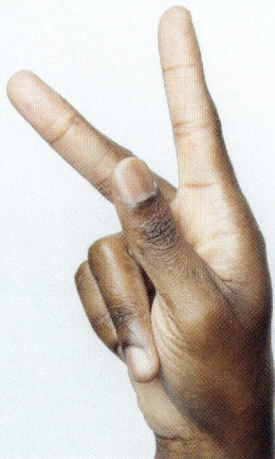

L

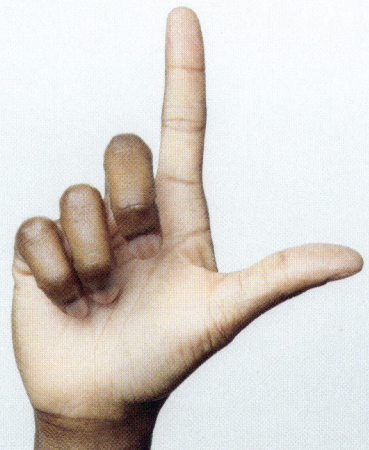

M

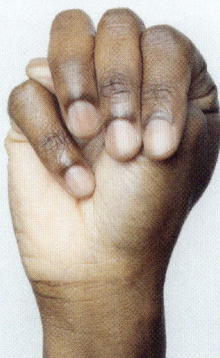

N

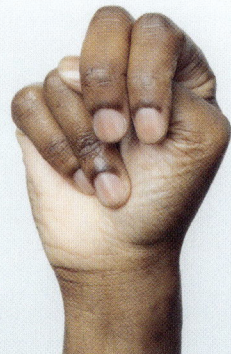

O

P

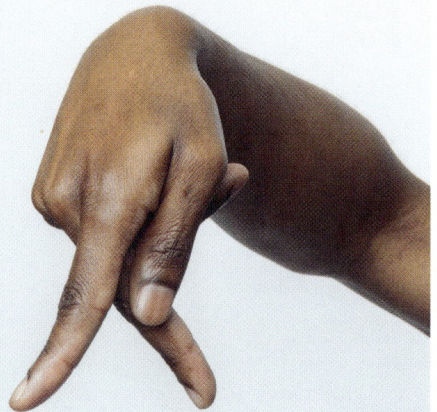

LEARN BLACK AMERICAN SIGN LANGUAGE

Q

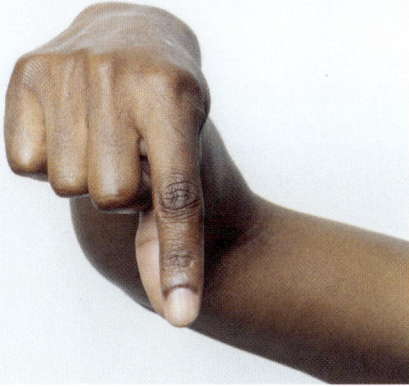

Q side view

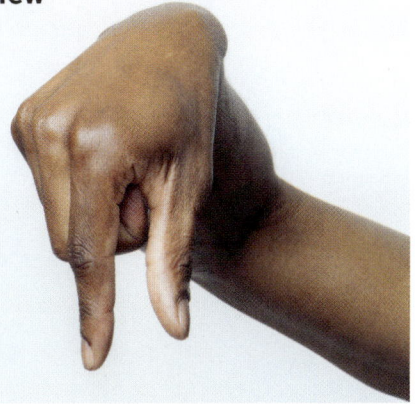

R

S

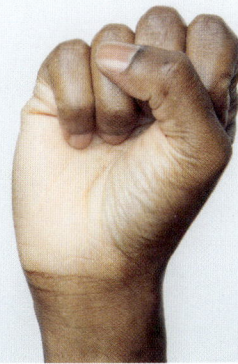

T

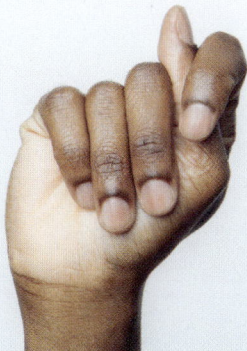

U

V

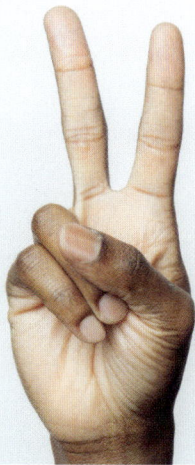

W

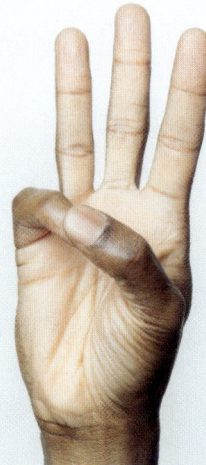

X

X side view

Y

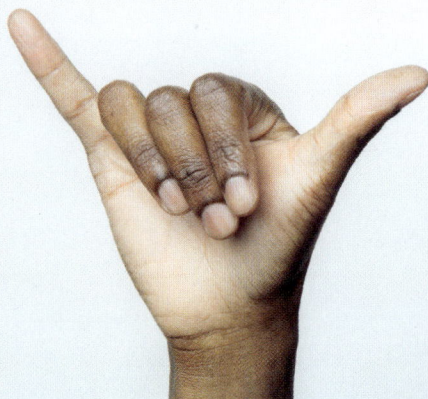

Z1

Z2

Z3

Z4

Franklin is signing the word *October* (page 42) and Stephanie is signing the word *dark* (page 46).

TIME & WEATHER

SUNDAY

HOME

Place both hands in a 5-handshape and touch the palms together twice.
Note: *This motion is similar to how Black people clap in church.*

ASL

Place both hands in a flat 5-handshape facing the audience. Then move them in opposite circles toward each other.

SATURDAY

Place your index finger to the side of your cheek and tap your cheek.

MONDAY

HOME

Use a mouth movement for "Monday" while pointing your index finger at your cheek.

TUESDAY

Touch your right index finger to the pad of the left middle finger. Make a mouth movement for "Tuesday."

WEDNESDAY

Curve the fingers of both hands and position the palms up. Then move them in inward circular motions. Make a mouth movement for "Wednesday."

THURSDAY

Touch the right index finger to the pad of the left hand's third finger. Make a mouth movement for "Thursday."

FRIDAY

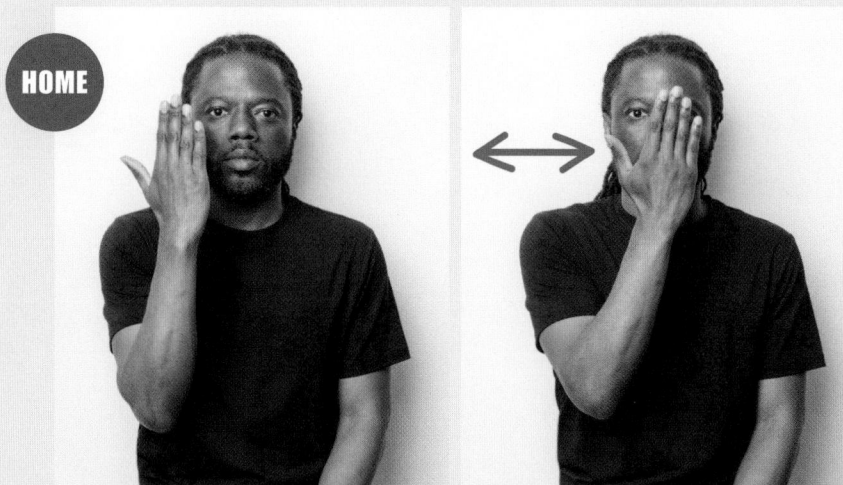

Place your hand flat, with the four fingers together and the thumb extended (flat B-handshape, page 22). With the palm facing you, move it from left to right.

TODAY

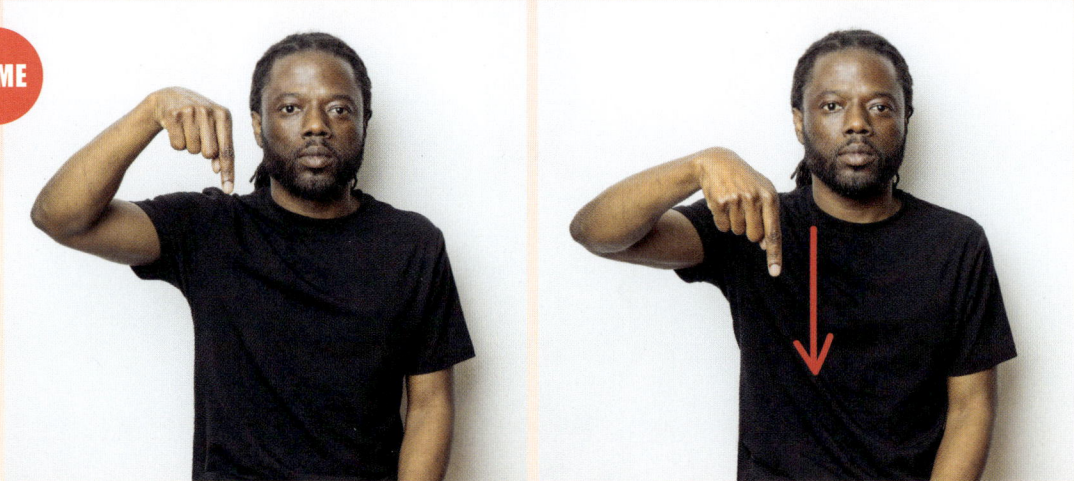

With your index finger, point downward repeatedly.
Note: Use your facial expression to indicate a sense of urgency.

TOMORROW

Start with your index finger pointing down. Then trace an arc from side to side.
Note: The difference between yesterday and tomorrow is the facial expression and mouthing. For tomorrow, close one eye.

YESTERDAY

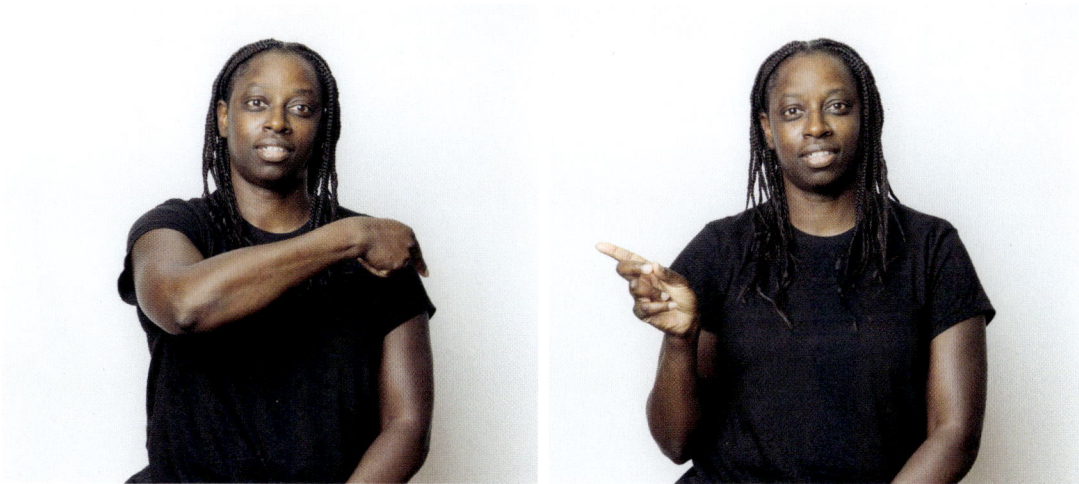

Point your index finger down and make an arc from side to side while raising your eyebrows.

SOON

HOME

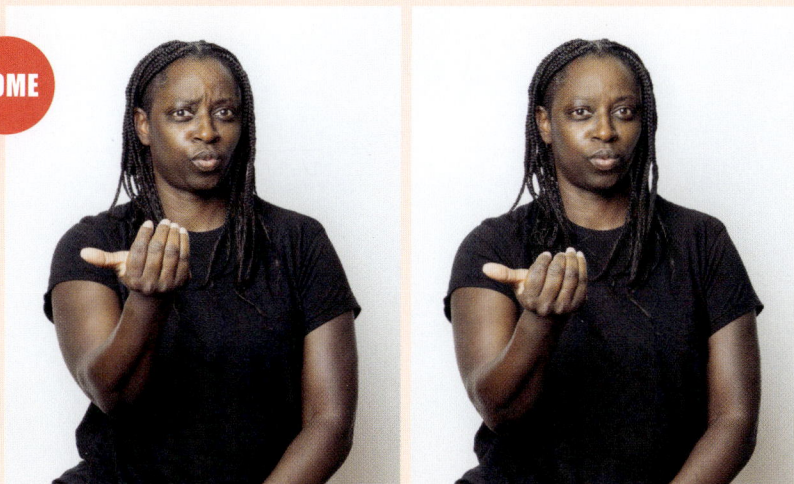

Place your hand curved with the four fingers together and the thumb extended (B-handshape, page 22). With the palm facing up, curl your fingers into your palm repeatedly in quick, small movements.

LONGTIME

Cross your arms at waist level and point the index fingers of both hands. Then open your arms until your fingers are pointing up.

REGULARLY

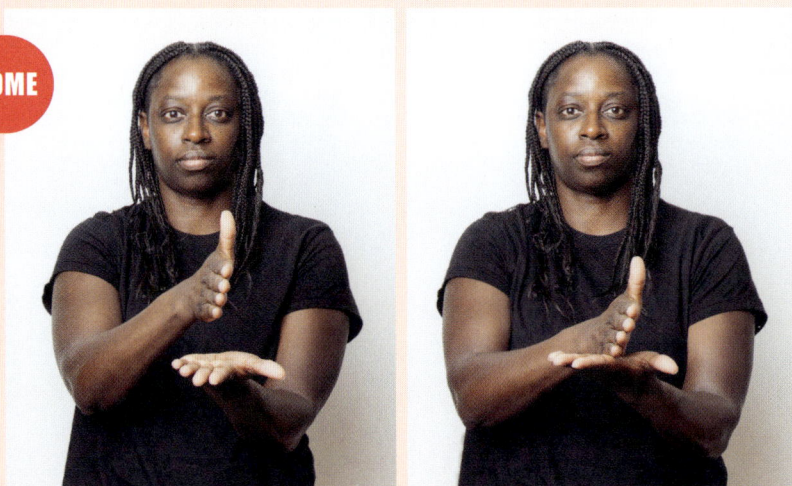

Place your left hand palm up. Place your right hand flat with the four fingers together and the thumb extended (B-handshape, page 22). Then tap the side of your right hand against your left palm twice.
Note: The sign is identical for frequently and same.

JANUARY

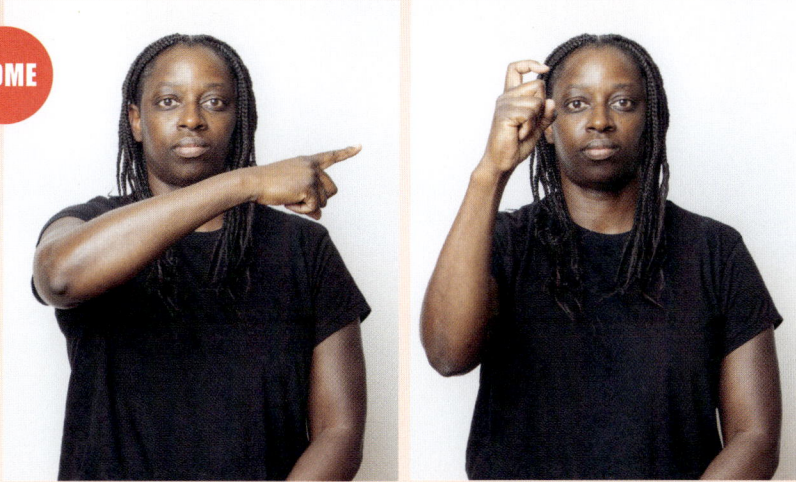

Point your index finger, then bend it up and down while moving in an arc from side to side.
Note: *The sign is the same for New Year's.*

FEBRUARY

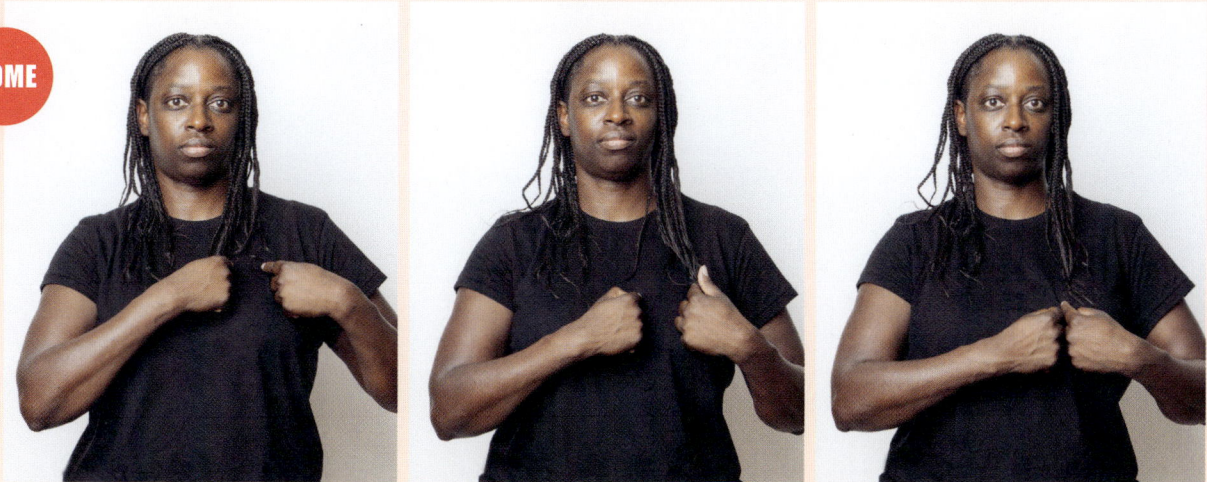

Touch your index fingers over your heart. Then draw the shape of a heart.
Note: *The sign is based on Valentine's Day.*

MARCH

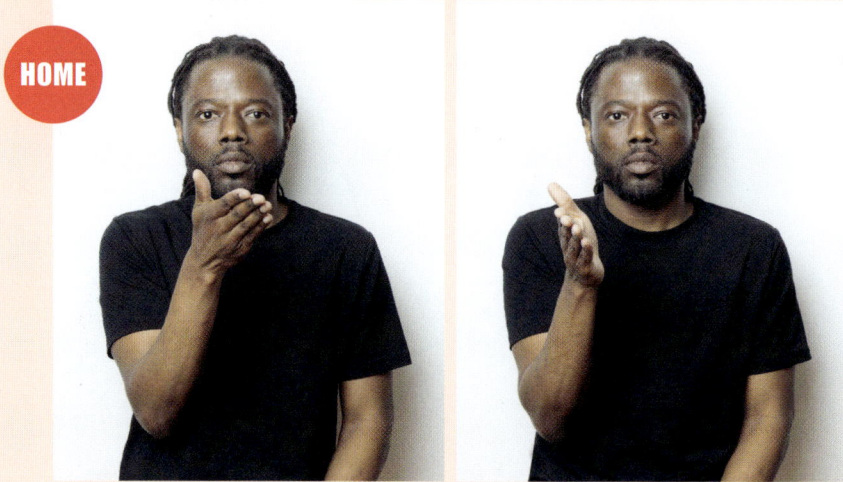

Place your hand flat, with the four fingers together and the thumb extended (flat B-handshape, page 22). With your hand at chest level and the thumb pointing up, move your hand from side to side.
Note: *The sign describes a characteristically windy month.*

APRIL

Make an oval with your index finger and thumb without touching each other. Place it over your eye.
Note: *The sign is similar to egg.*

MAY

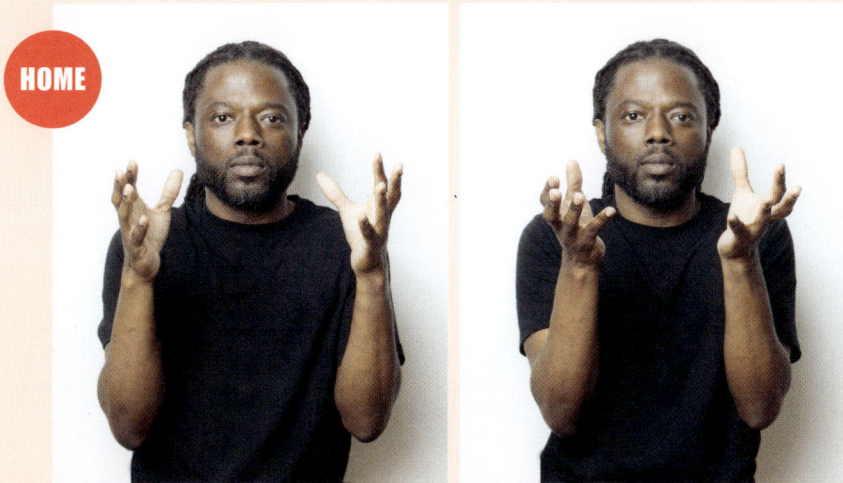

Place both hands in an open 5-handshape. Then curve both hands and make a quick half-twist movement.

JUNE

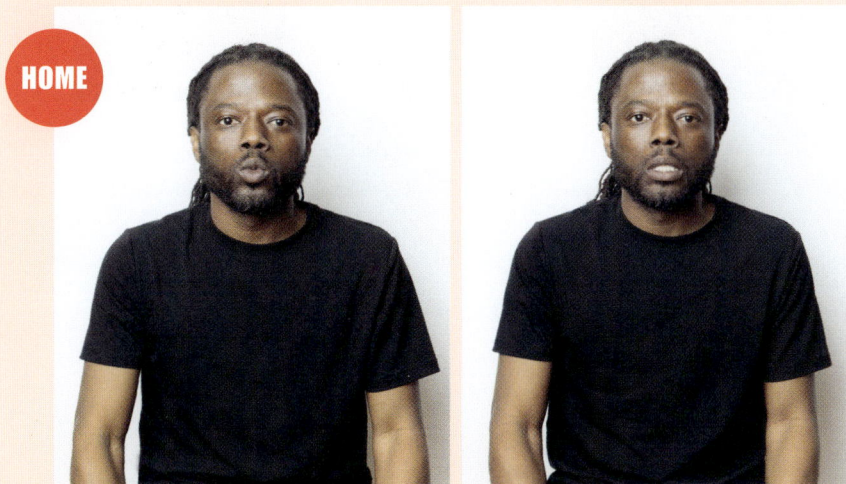

Use a mouth movement for "June."

JULY

Start with a straight index finger, then bend it up and down while moving in a small arc from side to side. Then form a fist and quickly open your hand while moving in a circle clockwise.

Note: The sign is the same for the Fourth of July.

AUGUST

HOME

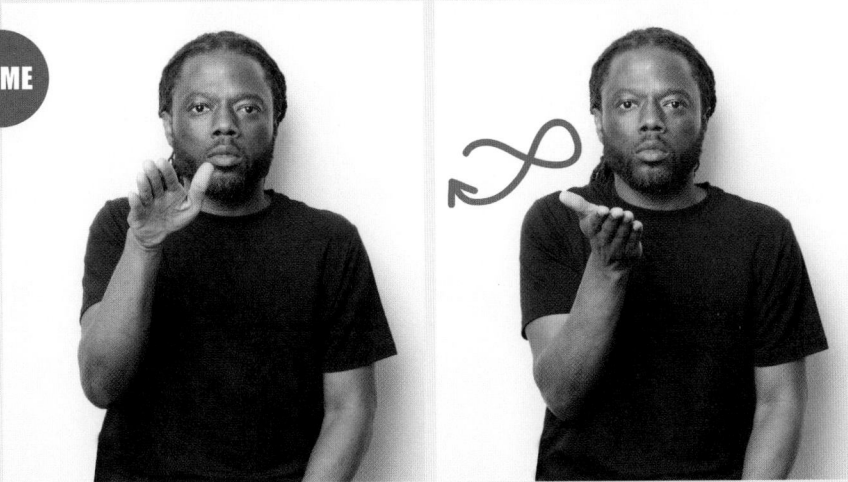

Place your hand flat, with the four fingers together and the thumb extended (flat B-handshape, page 22) at chest level. In a flopping motion, rotate your hand.

SEPTEMBER

HOME

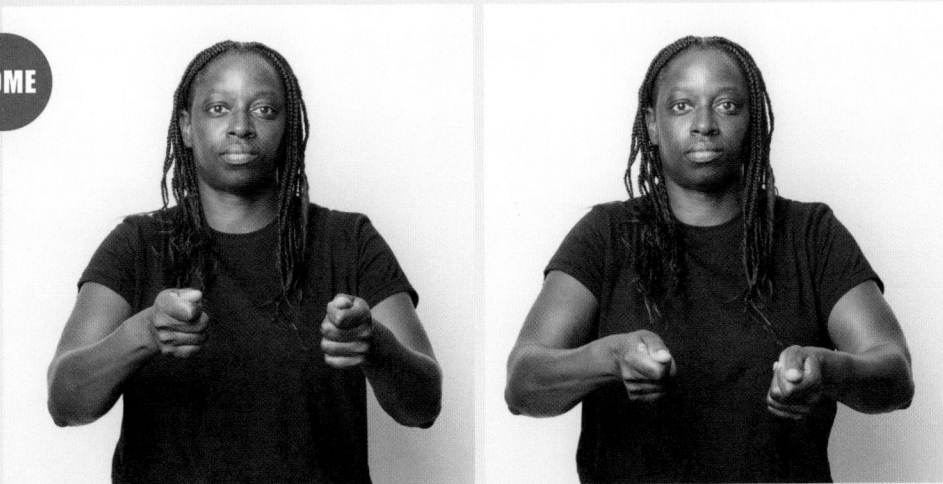

Place both your hands into fists and shake them forward toward your audience.

OCTOBER

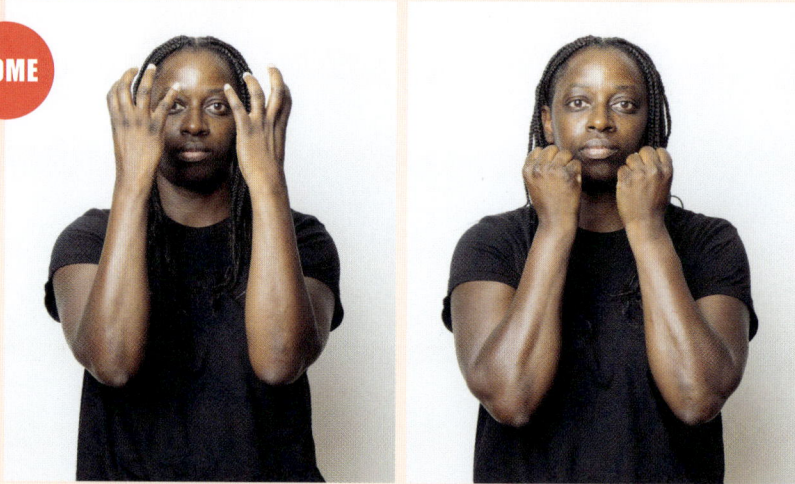

Place your hands at eye level with your fingers in a spread 5-handshape and the palms facing you. Then move your hands downward while curling the fingers together.
Note: *The sign is the same for Halloween.*

NOVEMBER

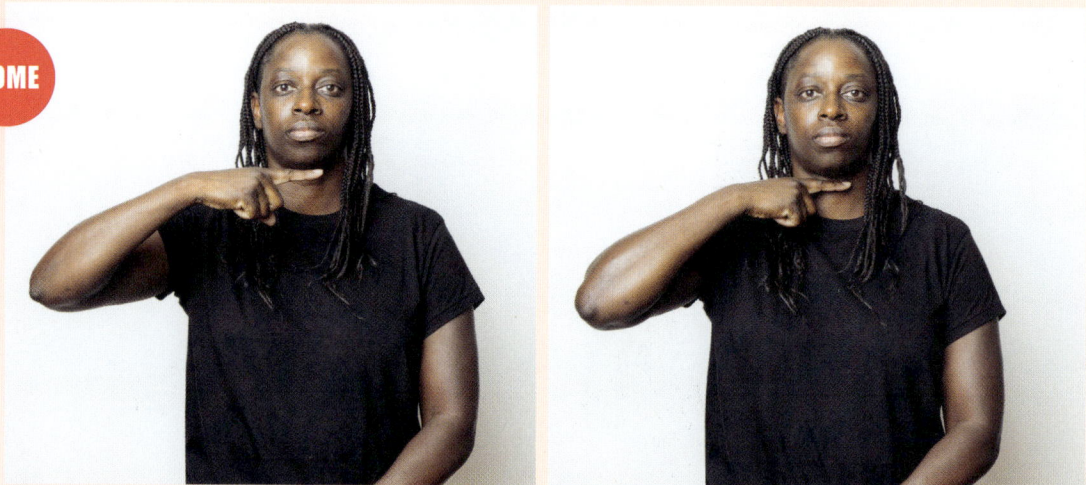

Place your index finger near your neck. Then tap the side of your finger against your neck twice in a quick, repetitive motion.
Note: *The sign is the same for Thanksgiving.*

DECEMBER

HOME

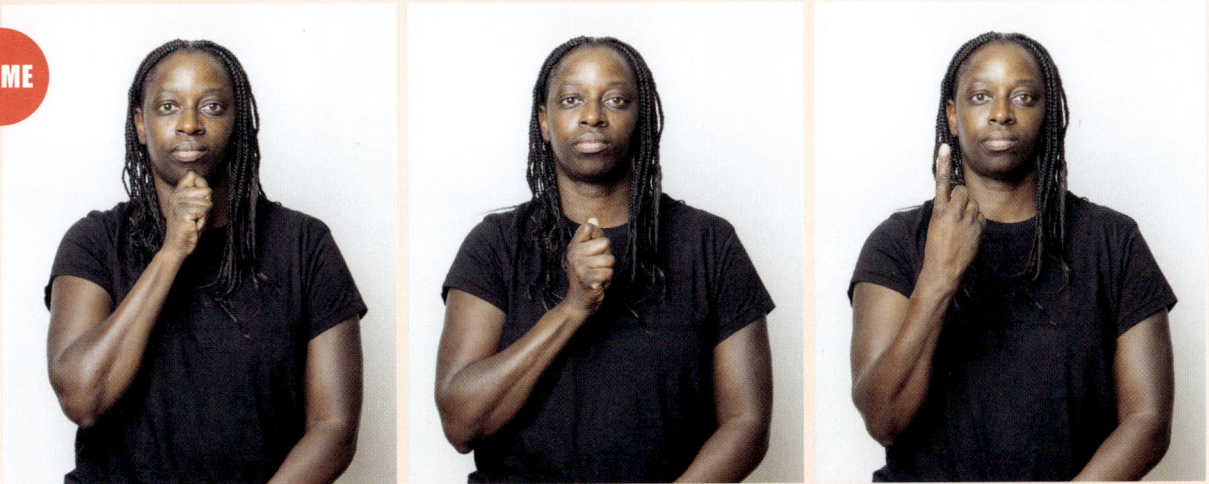

Place your hand at chin level, with the index finger bent, the thumb pointing up, and the bottom three fingers curled into a fist. Touch your index finger and thumb together repeatedly and move your hand as if you are stroking a beard. Then point your index finger up twice.
Note: The sign is the same for Christmas.

EASTER NORTH CAROLINA

Point the two first fingers of your right hand with the thumb underneath. Place your left hand in a 5-handshape with the fingers pointing up. Touch the right-hand fingers to the left palm, then pull the hands apart and move your fingers in an arch toward to the audience.

MORNING

HOME

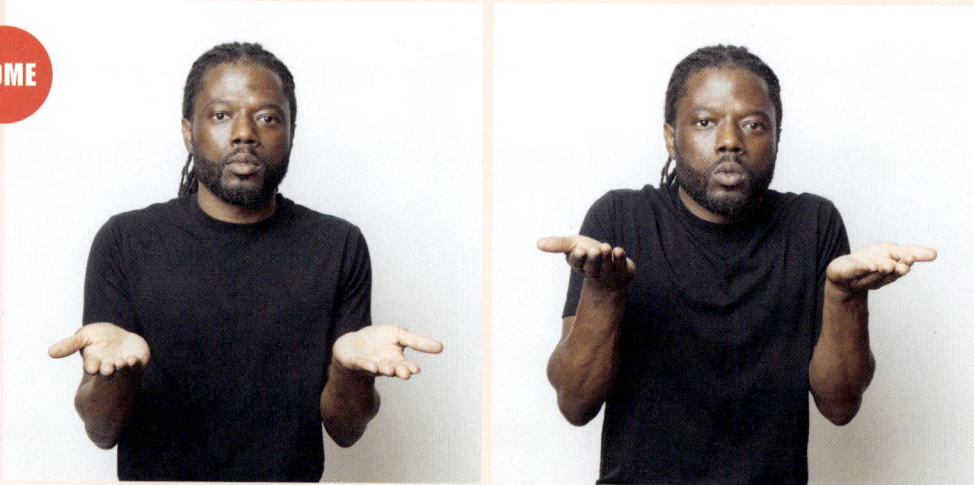

Place both hands palm up, then move them upward.
Note: The sign describes the morning sunrise.

ASL

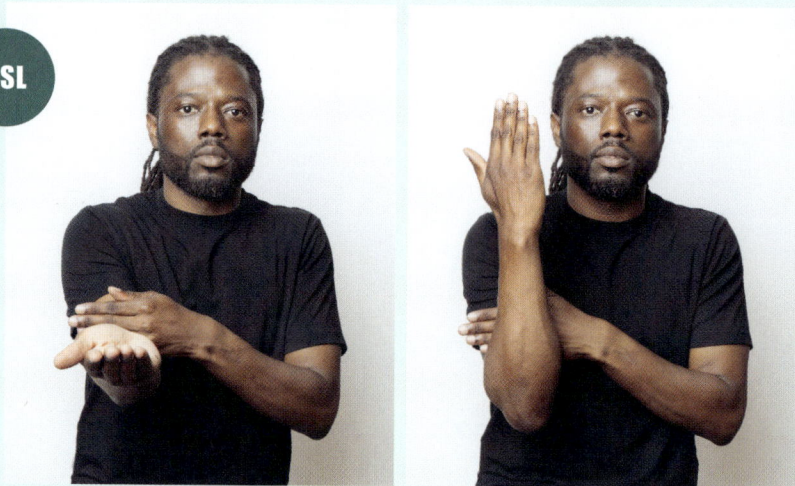

Place both hands in a 5-handshape with the right arm extended in front of you and the left hand resting at the elbow. With the right palm facing up, raise your forearm so your hand moves toward your face.

NIGHT

Place your hand above your head, with the palm facing down and your fingers slightly curved. Then, with a loose wrist, swing your hand down.
Note: *Keep this action light, as if night is "falling."*

MOON

Make a C shape with your index finger and thumb, with the rest of the fingers curled. Place your hand near your head and move it upward.

DARK

Place both hands in a 5-handshape above your head with the palms facing down. Then move your hands down.

BRIGHT

Hold your hands spread in front of you. Then move your hands upward in arcs going in opposite directions.
Note: *The sign describes the light outside.*

COLD

HOME

Place both hands in a fist and shake them slightly while making a scrunched up facial expression that signifies being cold.

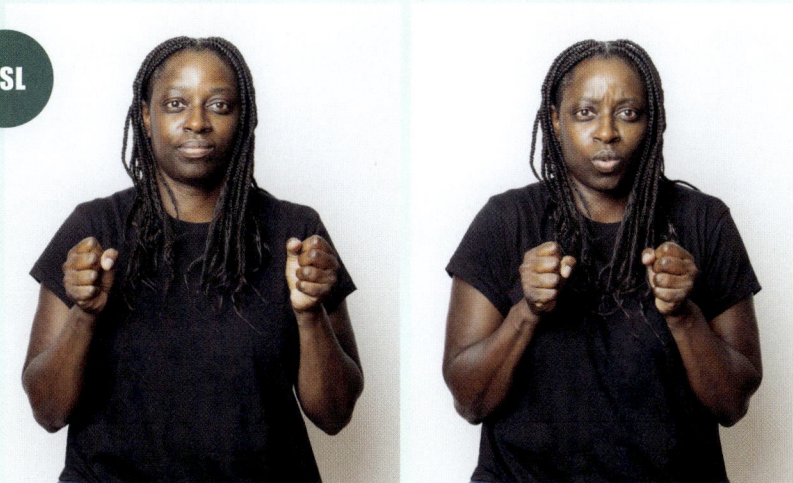

ASL

Place both hands in a fist (S-handshape, page 25) with the palms facing inward. Move both hands in and out in the neutral space.

HOT

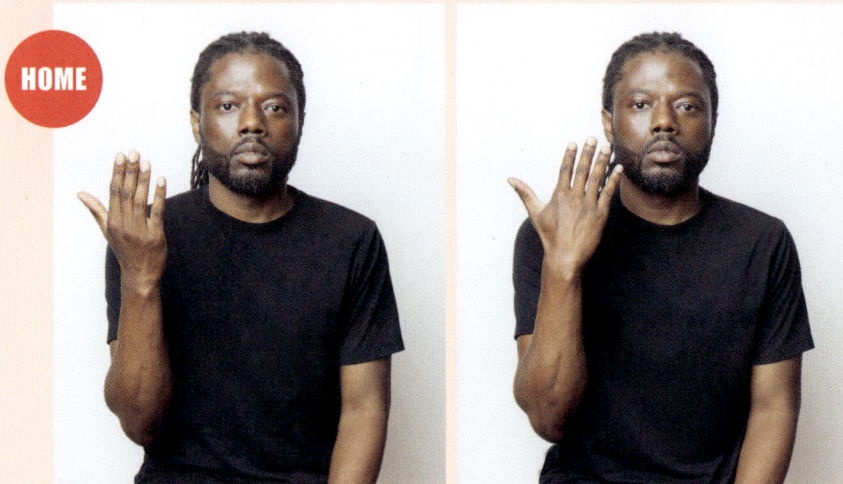

HOME

Place your hand in a 5-handshape with the palm facing you. Then wave your hand toward your face like you're fanning yourself.

WARM

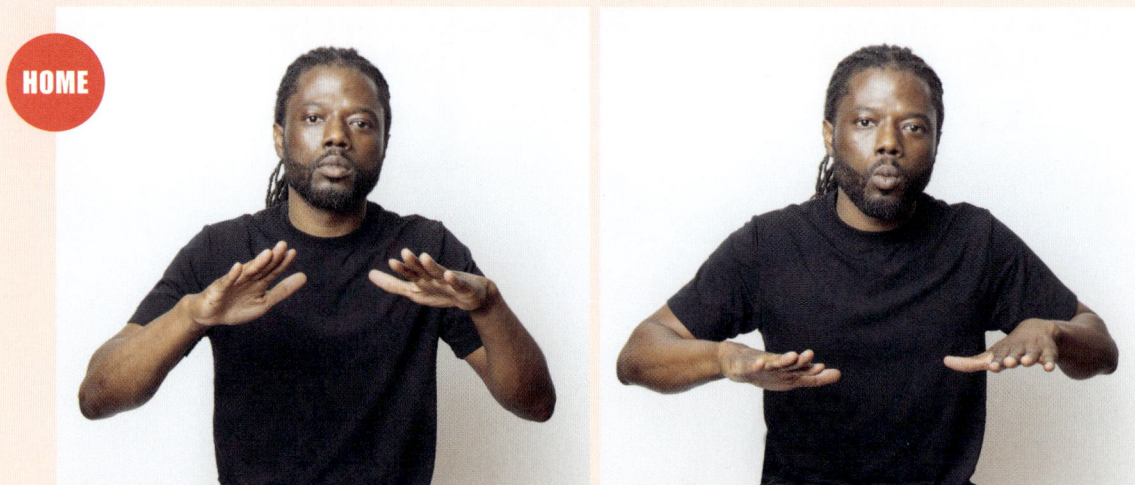

HOME

Place both hands with the fingers spread in a 5-handshape and the palms facing down. Start with the thumbs touching and then move them slowly apart to the sides.

WINDY

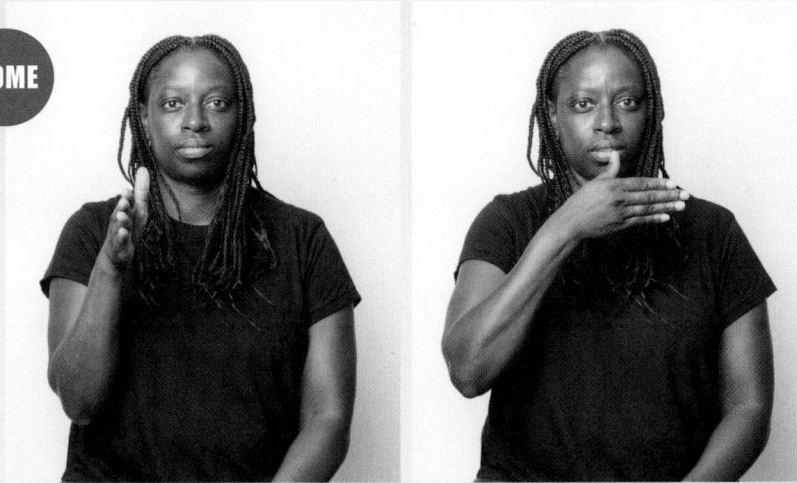

Place your hand in a 5-handshape with the palm facing the side. Then swing the hand side to side.

STORM

Place your hand in a 5-handshape. Swing the hand quickly left and right with a "storm" mouth movement.
Note: The sign is similar to windy, but for storm your hand should move with more force.

Franklin is signing the word *boy* while Stephanie is signing the word *girl* (page 59).

FAMILY & FRIENDS

PAPA

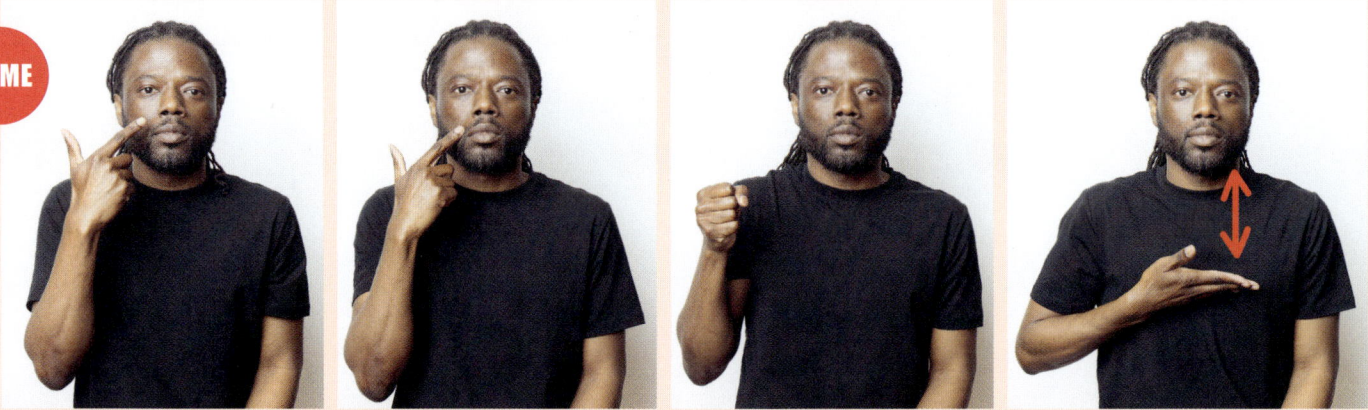

HOME

Point the index finger at the side of the mustache area twice, then make a fist at chest level. Then place your hand flat, with the four fingers together and the thumb extended (flat B-handshape, page 22) at the middle of your chest and move it up and down.

MOM

HOME

Place your hand curved like a cup at the side of your chest with the palm facing up. Move your hand up and down repeatedly.

SISTER

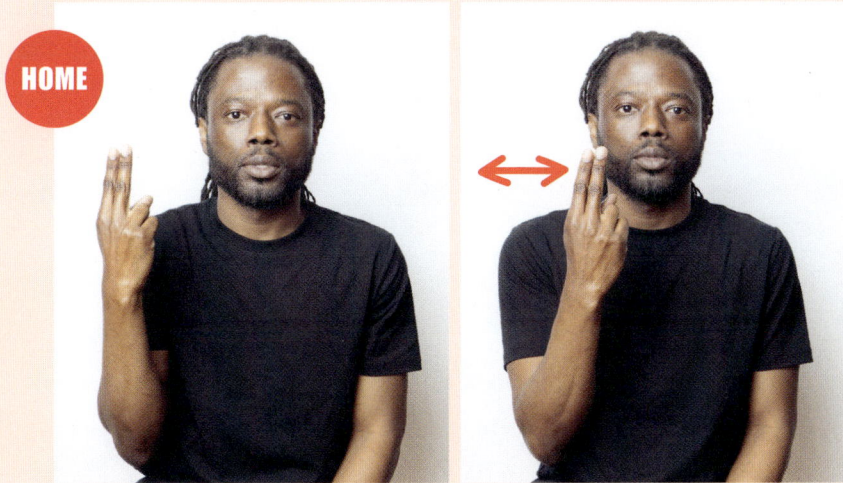

Point your index and middle fingers up, with the rest of the fingers curled (U-handshape, page 25) and the palm facing you. Move your hand side to side twice and make a "sister" mouth movement.

BROTHER

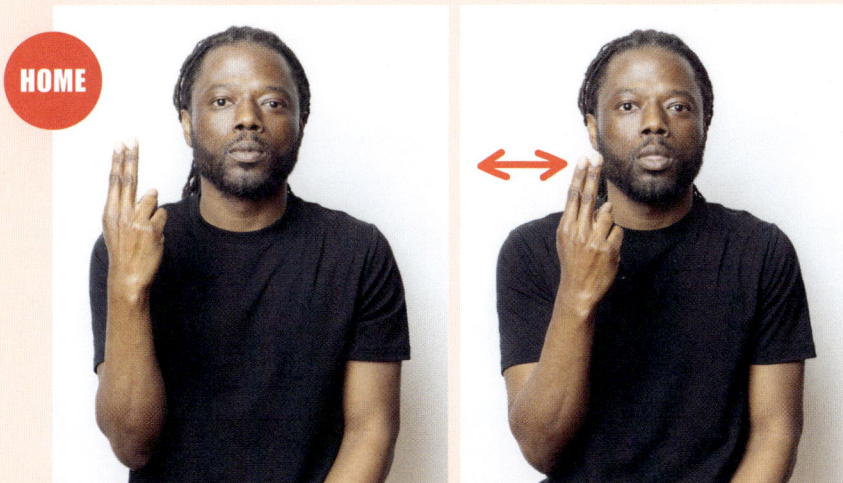

Point your index and middle fingers up, with the rest of the fingers curled (U-handshape, page 25) and the palm facing you. Move your hand side to side twice and make a "brother" mouth movement.

TWIN

HOME

Sign the number "two" by pointing the index and middle fingers up and spread apart. Then make a 5-handshape with both hands at chest level and the fingers slightly overlapped. Move your hands up and down twice in the chest area with short movements.

BABY

HOME

Place your hand flat, with the four fingers together and the thumb extended (flat B-handshape, page 22). With the palm facing up, move your hand up and down twice in the chest area with short movements.

GRANDMA

HOME

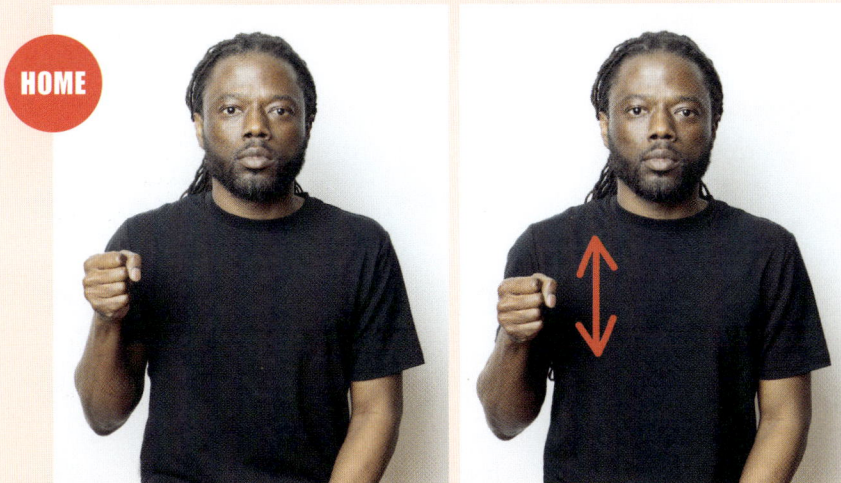

Place your hand in a fist (S-handshape, page 25), with the thumb on top of your knuckles. Then move your hand up and down.

GRANDPA

HOME

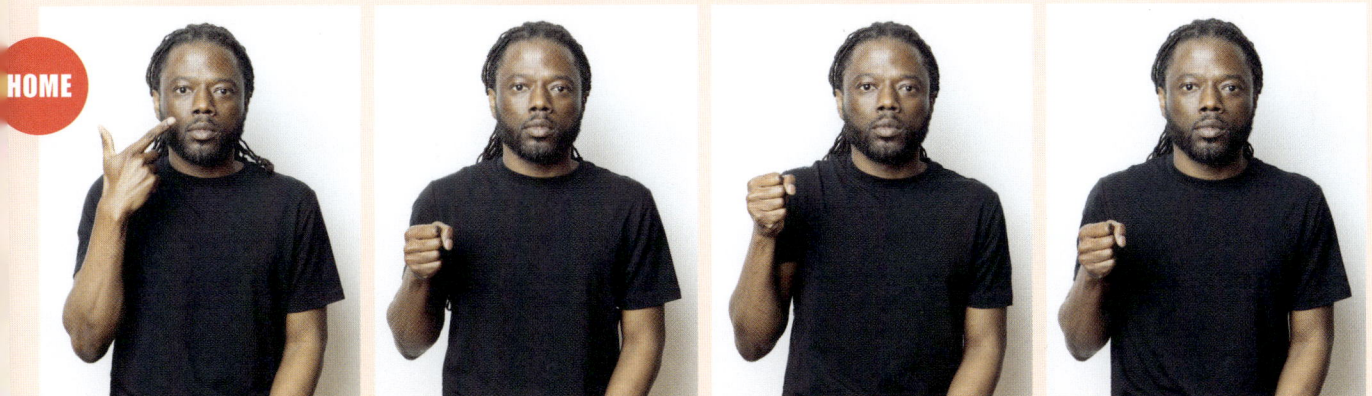

Point the index finger and drag it twice along the mustache area. Then make a fist (S-handshape, page 25) and move it up and down.

COUSIN TEXAS

Place both index fingers at the sides of your waist pointing down. Then move your hands to chest level in the neutral space and touch the sides of the fingers together.

Curve the fingers of your hand to make a C shape (C-handshape, page 22) on the side of your cheek, then rotate it forward and backward.

FRIEND

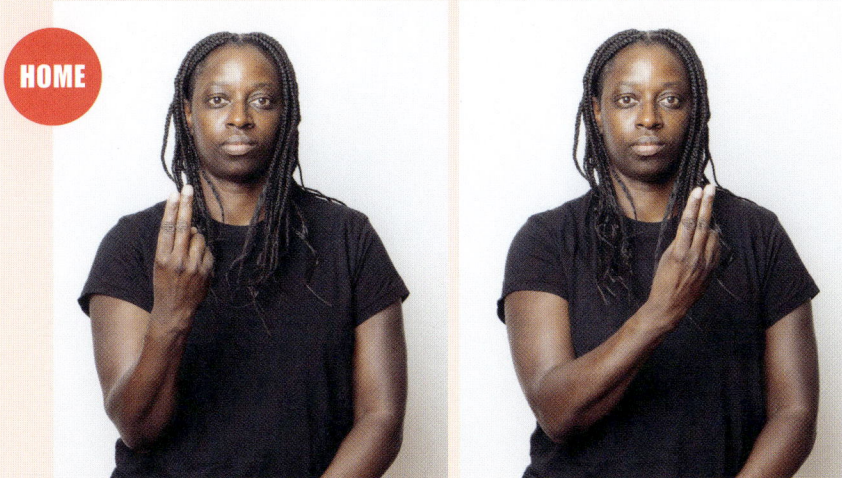

Point your index and middle fingers up, with the rest of the fingers curled (U-handshape, page 25) and the palm facing you. Move your hand sideways twice and make a "friend" mouth movement.

Hook your index fingers together, then switch sides and flip your hands before hooking your fingers again.

GIRLFRIEND

HOME

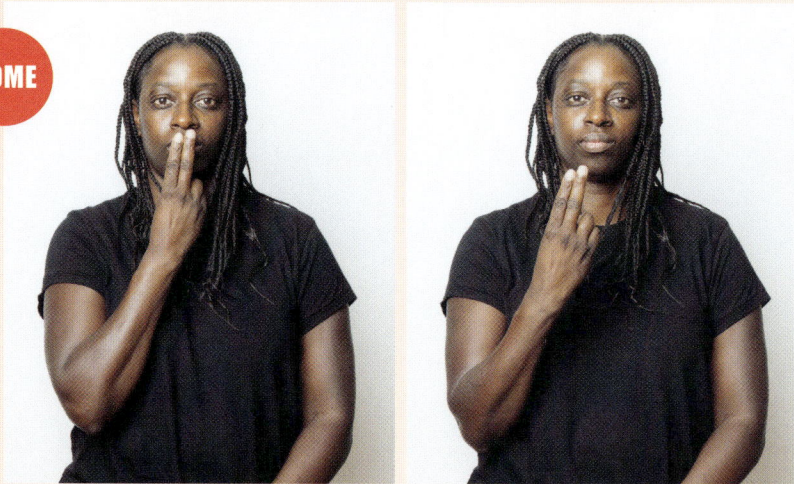

Point your index and middle fingers up, with the rest of the fingers curled (U-handshape, page 25) and the palm facing you. Touch your lips, then move your hand toward the audience with a "girlfriend" mouth movement.

BOYFRIEND

HOME

Point your index and middle fingers up, with the rest of the fingers curled (U-handshape, page 25) and the palm facing you. Tap your fingers twice against your lips with a "boyfriend" mouth movement.

GIRL

HOME

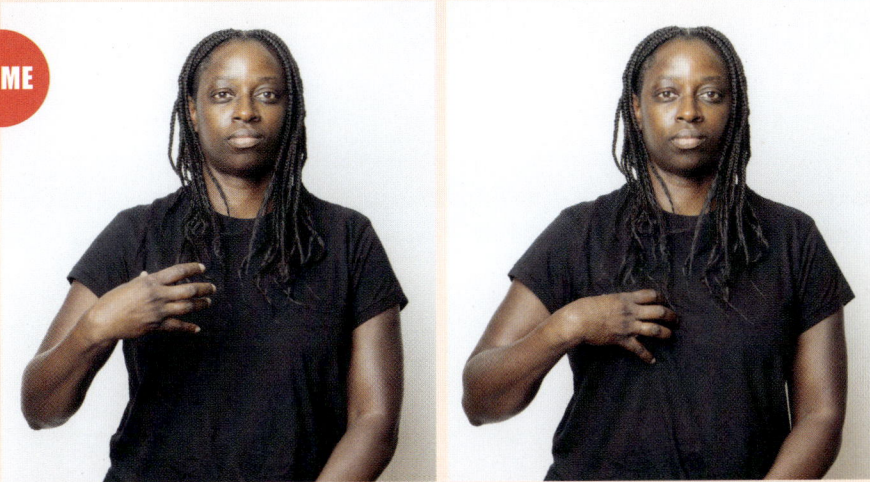

Place your hand in a curved 5-handshape. Tap your fingers against the side of your chest twice.

BOY

HOME

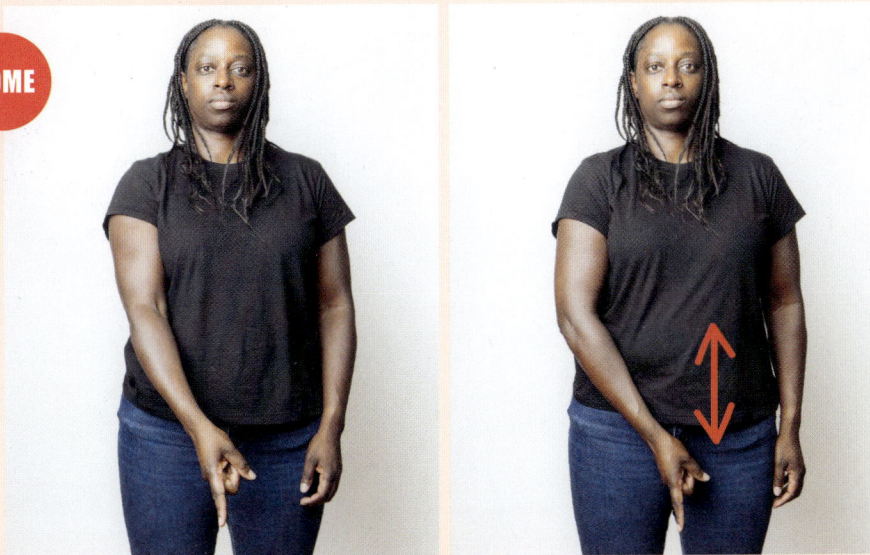

Point your index finger down in a handshape for the number one. Then move your hand up and down below the lower abdomen.

Franklin is signing the BASL Texas variation of the word *movie* while Stephanie is signing the BASL Arkansas variation (page 77).

DAILY LIFE

WORK

Place your hand in a 5-handshape, with the thumb extended, and place your thumb at your armpit. Then lift your elbow up and down repeatedly.

MEETING

Point your thumb and index finger and place your hand in front of your nose. Then move your hand from side to side using quick, repetitive motions.

TEACHER

Touch the fingers of each hand together (flat O-handshape, page 24). Place your fingers at the sides of your head at forehead level and move them forward. Then spread the fingers of both hands into a 5-handshape with the palms facing each other and move them down to about chest level.

TEACHER

Touch the fingers of each hand together (flat O-handshape, page 24). Place your fingers at the sides of your head at chin level and move them forward. Then spread the fingers of both hands into a 5-handshape with the palms facing each other and move them down to about chest level.

PRINCIPAL NORTH CAROLINA

Place the left hand flat and upright, with the thumb extended (flat B-handshape, page 22). Then point the index and middle fingers of the right hand and place your thumb between them (P-handshape, page 24). Move the right hand in an arc, starting above the left hand and ending at the palm of the left hand.

SCHOOL

Place your hands in a 5-handshape in front of your face, with the palms facing you. Then move your hands from side to side in a quick motion.

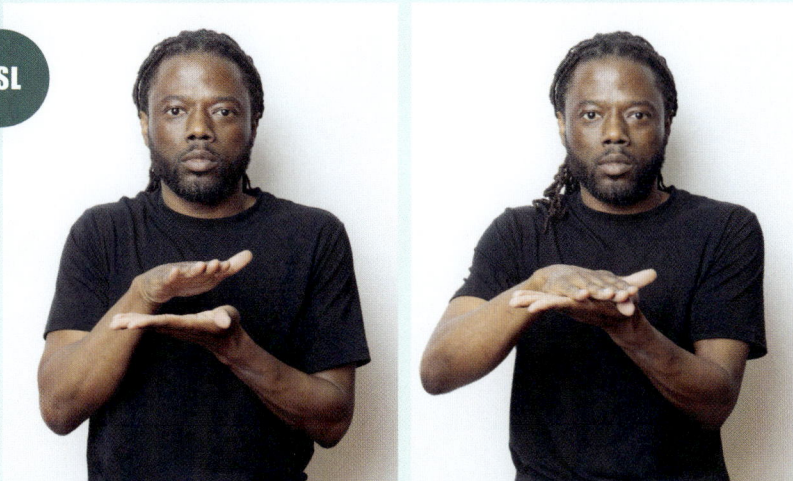

Place your hands in a 5-handshape horizontal, with one on top of the other and the palms facing each other. Touch the palms together twice.

RESTROOM VIRGINIA

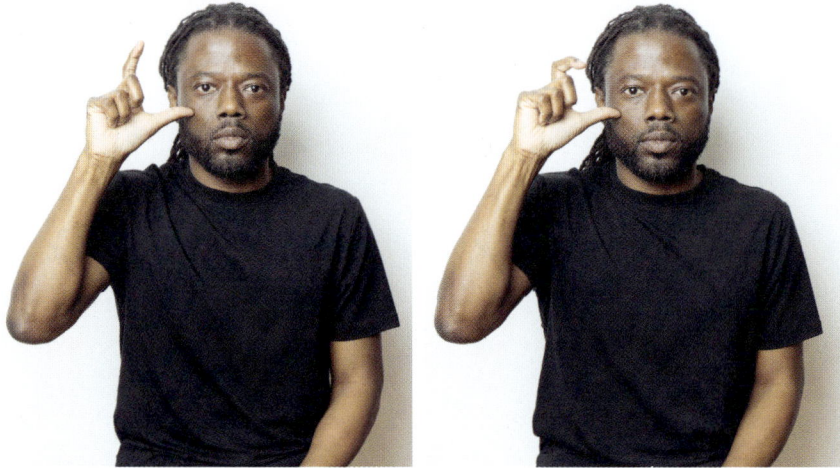

Place your hand at forehead level. Rest your thumb against the side of your face and point your index finger up with the palm facing the audience. Quickly bend your index finger up and down, as if pressing the shutter of a disposable camera.

YARD NORTH CAROLINA

Place both hands in a fist and turn the hand so the thumb is resting on top (A-handshape, page 22). Touch your knuckles together and then pull the right hand away from the left hand.

PREACHER NORTH CAROLINA

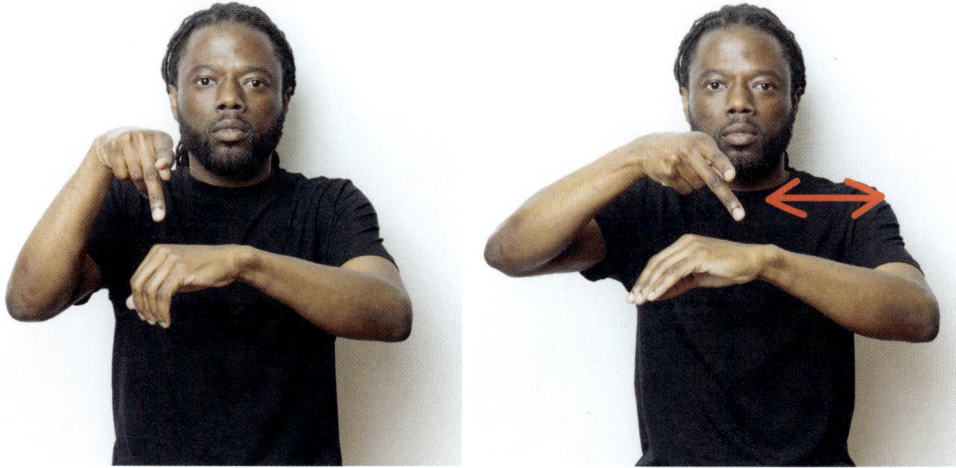

Place your left hand palm facing down with the fingers slightly curved. Then extend the index and middle fingers of your right hand and place your thumb between them (P-handshape, page 24). Swing the right hand back and forth above the left hand.

CHURCH

HOME

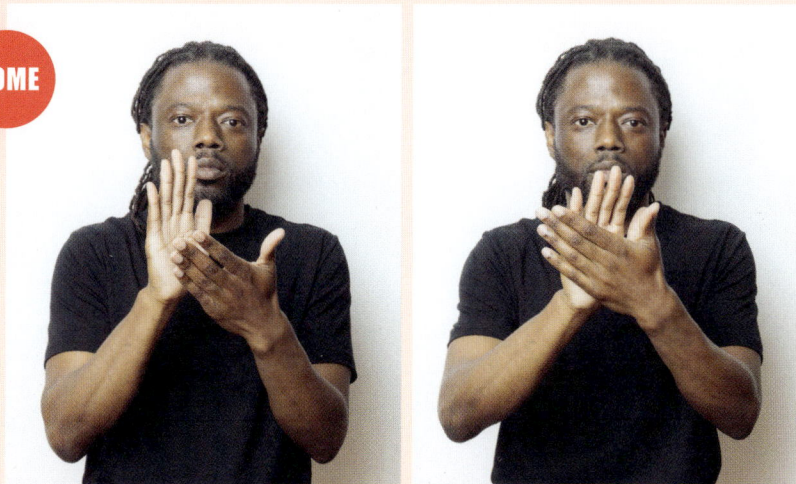

Place your hands at chest level with the palms facing each other. Then clap your right hand to your left.

CHOIR

Place both hands curved, with the four fingers together and the thumb extended (flat B-handshape, page 22). With the palms facing up, hold your hands at chin level and swing them left and right.

WEDDING

Place your hands in a 5-handshape on top of your head and drag them down to the shoulders.
Note: *The sign is the same for married.*

HOSPITAL NORTH CAROLINA

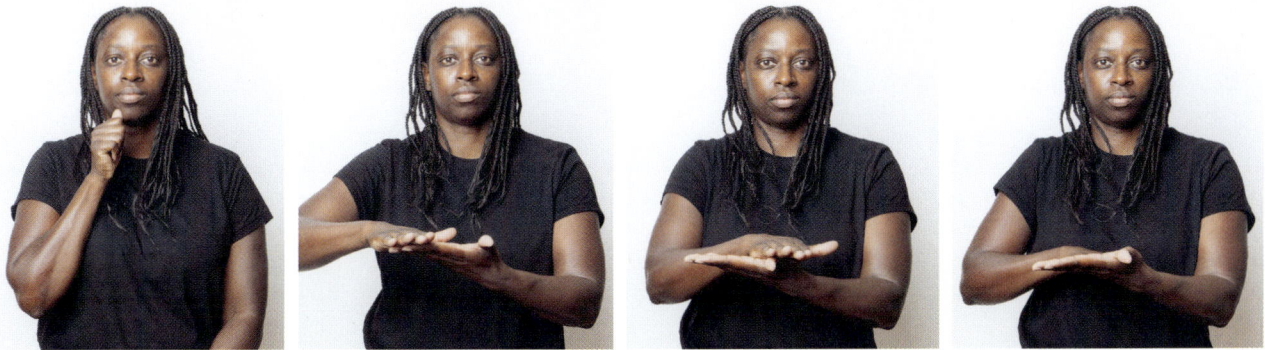

Place your right hand in a fist with the thumb pointed up (A-handshape, page 22) and touch the side of your chin with your thumb. Then make both hands a 5-handshape. Hold the left hand palm up and move the right palm in a circular motion on top.

AMBULANCE

HOME

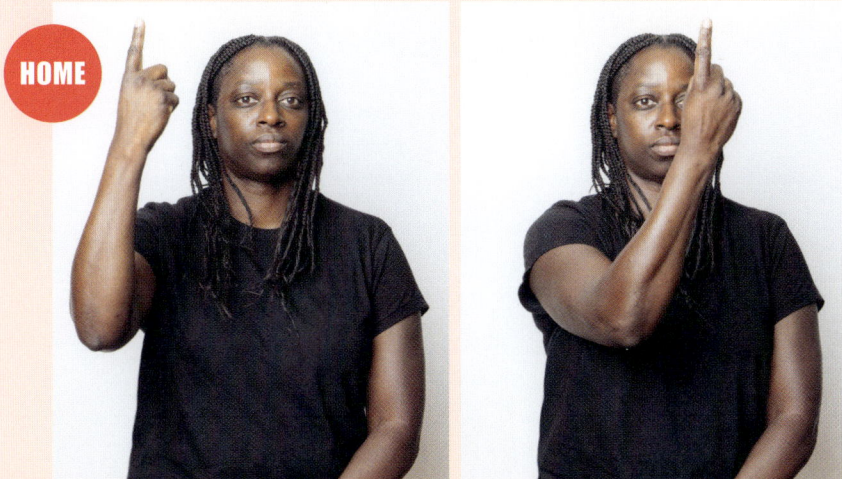

Point your index finger up near your head and move it in two big circular motions. Make a mouth movement for "ambulance."

POLICE

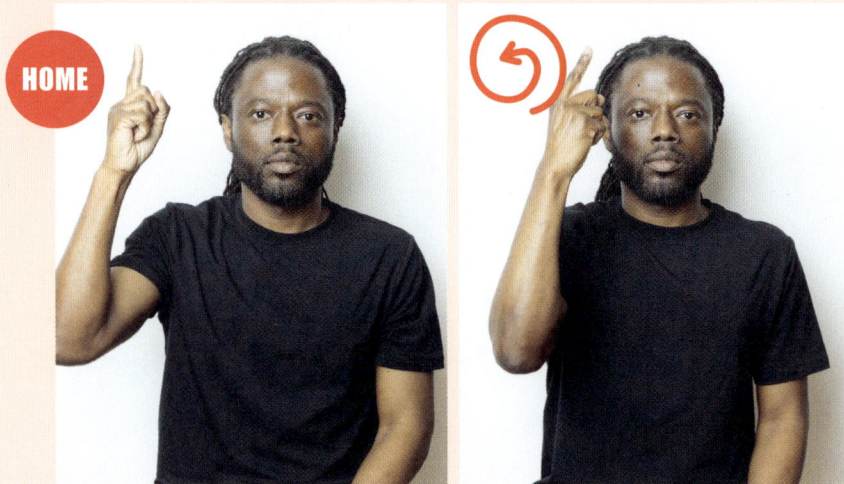

Point your index finger up near your head and move it in two small circular motions.

TRAIN

Place your fist at chest level with the hand turned so the thumb is toward your body. Then move it forward and back in a small circle, as if you're churning something.
Note: *Use a large motion for this sign.*

AIRPLANE

HOME

Place both hands flat at shoulder level and facing outward with the arm bent at the elbow. Then repeatedly move one arm up while the other moves down. Let your upper body tilt with the movement.

STORE ARKANSAS

Place the left arm horizontal across the chest with your hand in a fist. Then make a fist with your right hand but place your thumb between your index and middle fingers (T-handshape, page 25). Tap the side of the right hand against the left arm twice: below the wrist and near the elbow.

HAIR SALON TEXAS

Place both hands curved with the four fingers together and the thumb extended (flat B-handshape, page 22). Place them near the sides of the head with the palms facing you, but do not make contact with your head. Then move one hand forward and the other hand back a few times.

WIG

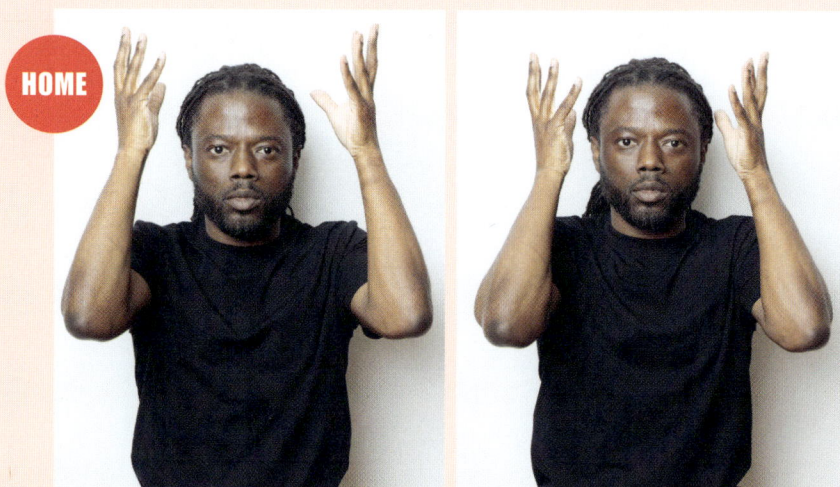

HOME

Place both hands in a 5-handshape with the fingers spread and slightly curved. Hold your hands at the sides of your head with the palms facing you and move them up and down twice. *Note: The sign describes how to place a wig on your head.*

LEARN BLACK AMERICAN SIGN LANGUAGE

WEAVE

Place the four spread fingers of your hand to the side of your head and using quick, repetitive movements, tap your fingers against your head.

BEACH

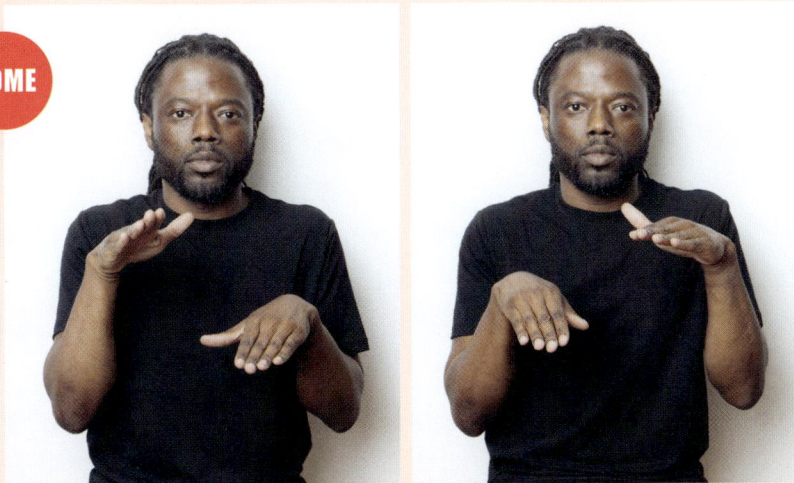

Place your hands flat, with the four fingers together and the thumb extended (flat B-handshape, page 22). Then rotate both hands in a forward motion alternating circles.
Note: *The sign mimics swimming.*

BLANKET

HOME

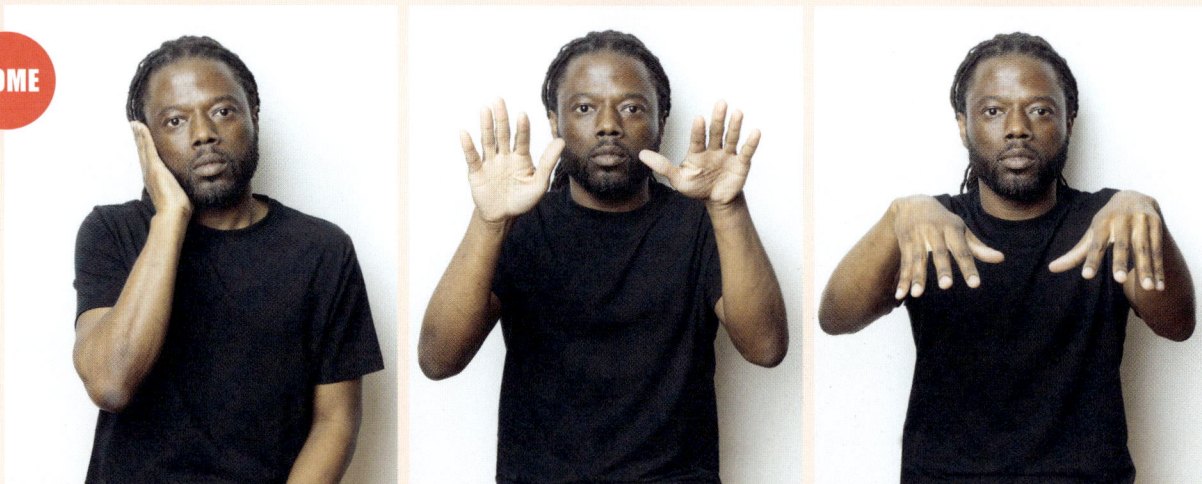

Place your right hand with four fingers flat and the thumb extended (B-handshape, page 22) and cup the side of your face. Then, with both hands in a 5-handshape, start at forehead level and move your hands down in an arch.

TOWEL

HOME

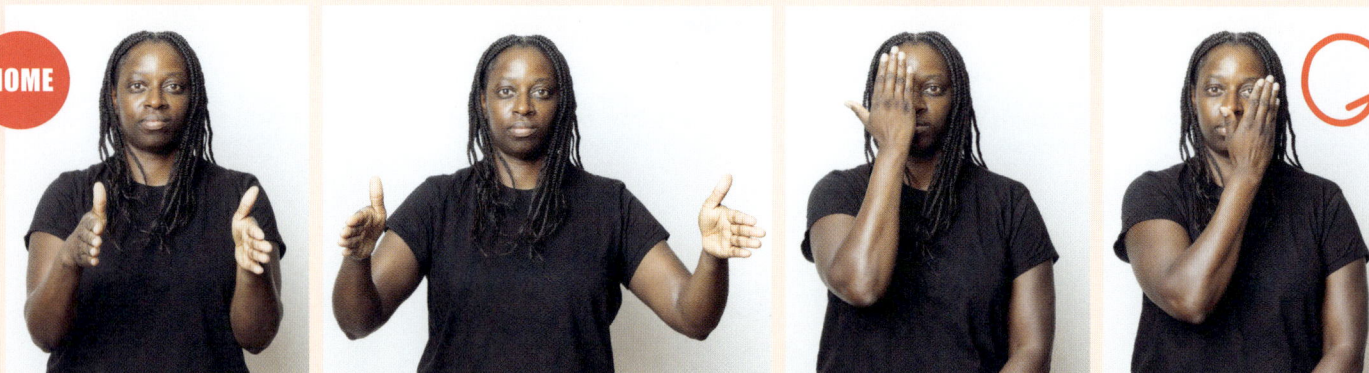

Place both hands flat, with the four fingers together and the thumb extended (flat B-handshape, page 22). Hold your hands in the neutral space, with the palms facing each other, and move them apart horizontally. Then place your right hand in front of your face, with the palm facing you, and move your hand in a circle counterclockwise.

BANK

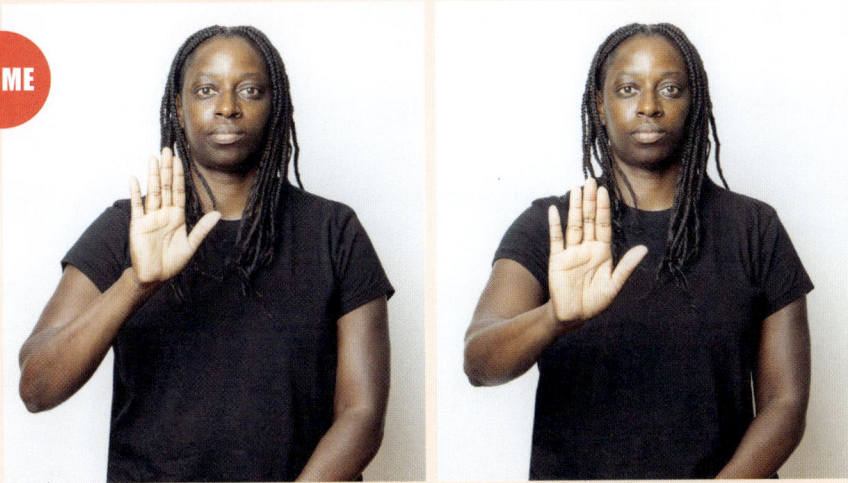

Place your right hand in the neutral space with your palm facing the audience. Then move it forward in a quick, repetitive movement.

CLUB

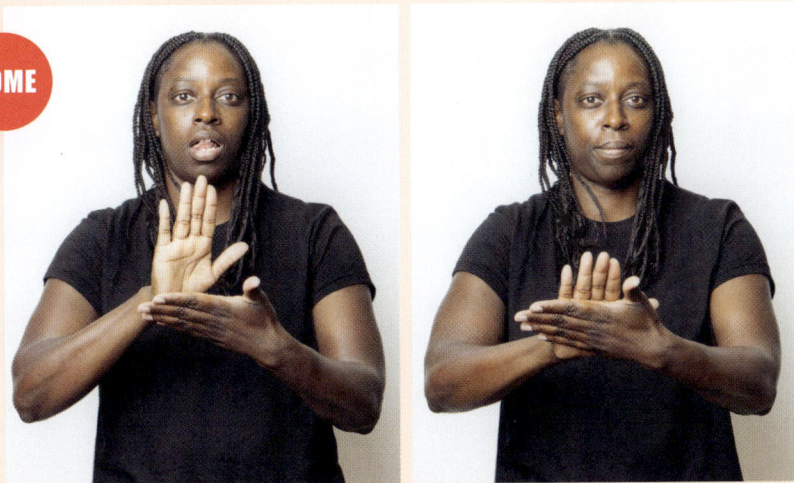

Place your hands at chest level with the palms facing each other and clap your right hand against your left.

BIRTHDAY

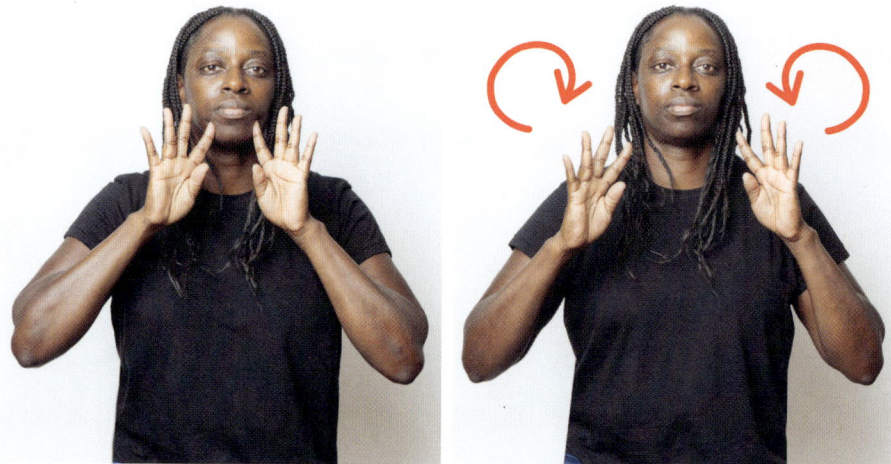

Place your hands near the sides of your face in a 4-handshape with your thumbs slightly bent. With the palms facing the audience, move your hands in small circles toward the middle.

DANCE

HOME

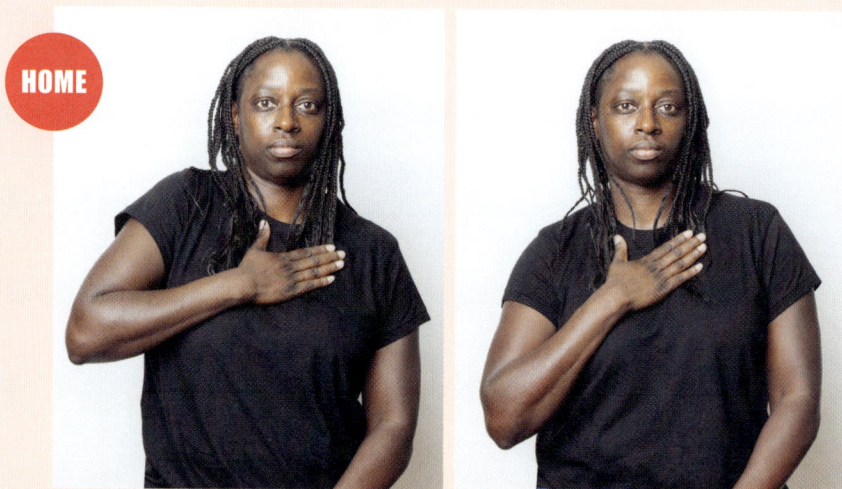

Place your hand over the middle of your chest, then alternate moving your shoulders up and down.

LEARN BLACK AMERICAN SIGN LANGUAGE

MOVIE ARKANSAS

Place your hand flat, with the four fingers together and the thumb extended (flat B-handshape, page 22). Then place your hand in front of your face horizontal, with your palm facing you, and move it up and down.

MOVIE TEXAS

Place both hands in a 5-handshape in the neutral space with the palms facing the audience and wave them.

HOME

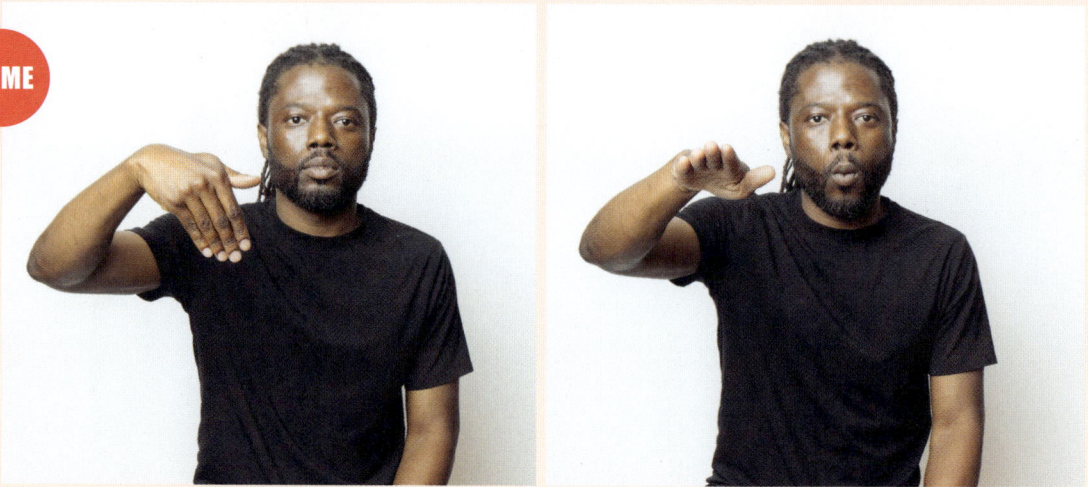

Place your hand flat, with the four fingers together and the thumb extended (flat B-handshape, page 22). Point the fingers down with the palm facing you, then sweep your hand upward until your hand is straight with a "home" mouth movement.

TRAILER

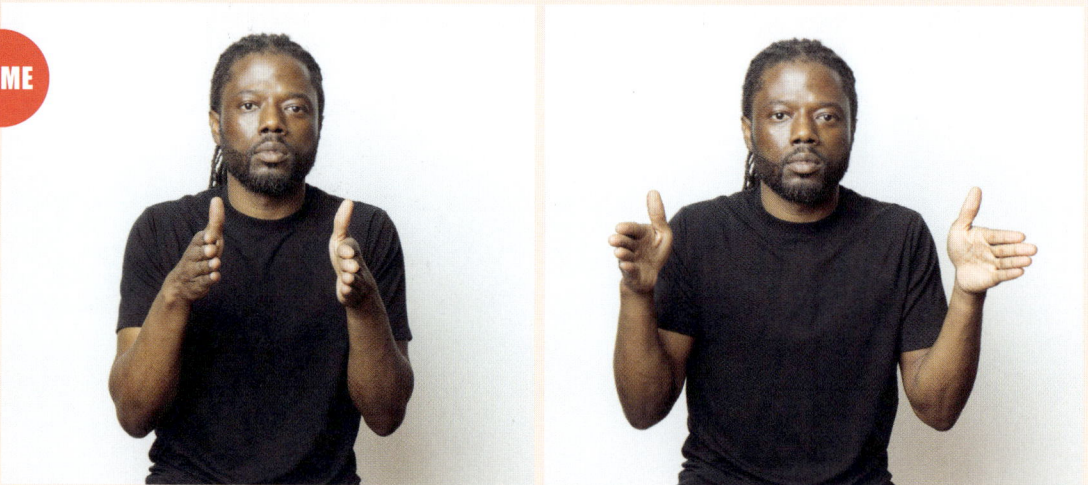

Place your hands flat, with the four fingers together and the thumb extended (flat B-handshape, page 22) with the palms facing each other. Then pull them apart.

DRYER

HOME

Point your index finger to the side, then draw a large circle in the air twice.
Note: The sign describes how the dryer movement looks.

LINE DRYING

HOME

Extend both index fingers and thumbs, with the other fingers curled, and point them down. Start with your hands close together in the neutral space, then move them out to the sides while opening and closing your fingers like you're pinching.
Note: The sign describes how clothes are placed on the line for drying.

WASHING MACHINE

HOME

Point your index finger down, then move it side to side in an arc twice.
Note: *The sign describes how the washing machine looks.*

ASL

Place both hands in a bent 5-handshape and hold them in the neutral space with the palms facing each other. Then make a twisting motion with your hands in opposite directions.

CLOTHES

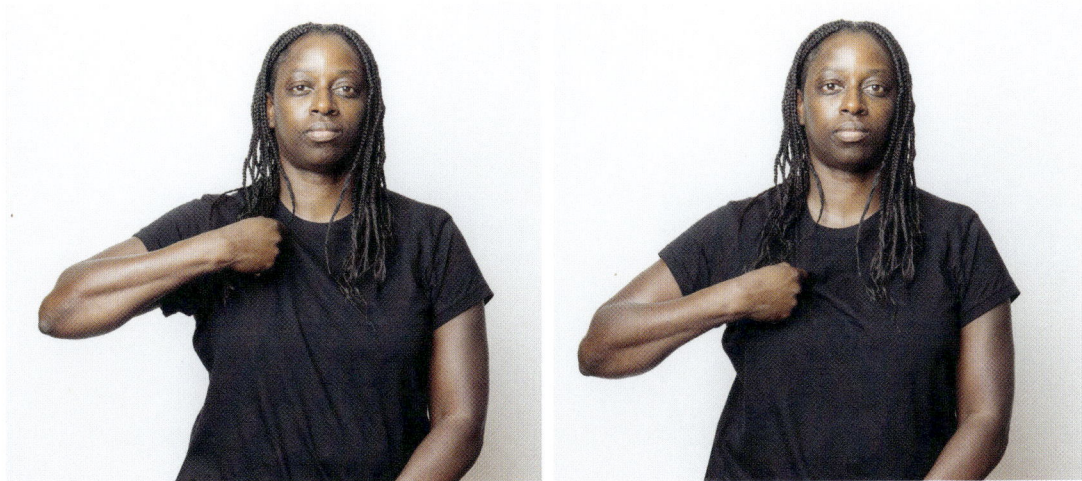

Pinch the index finger and thumb together, with the rest of the fingers closed. Then pinch the top you're wearing and move it up and down twice.

SOCKS VIRGINIA

Extend both index fingers. Point the left finger toward the audience and hold the right finger horizontal above. Then move the side of your right finger back and forth along the top of the left finger.

SHOES

HOME

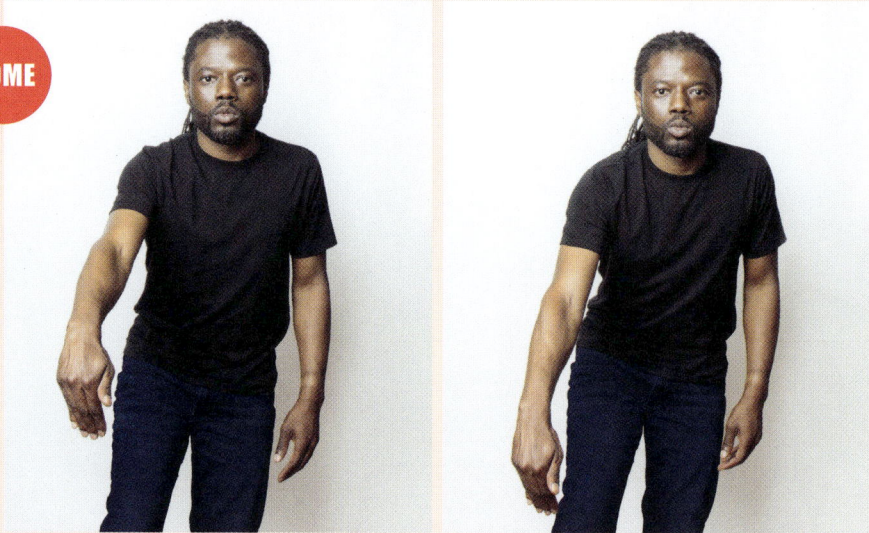

Place your hand slightly curved, with the four fingers together and the thumb extended (flat B-handshape, page 22) at your side. Point your fingers at your shoe and move your hand up and down.

EYEGLASSES

HOME

Curve both index fingers and thumbs around the sides of your eyes like an open nine. Then pull your hands out to the sides twice.

READING

Place your hands flat with the sides touching. Then hold them in front of your face with the palms facing you, and rock them in short side to side movements.

LIGHT

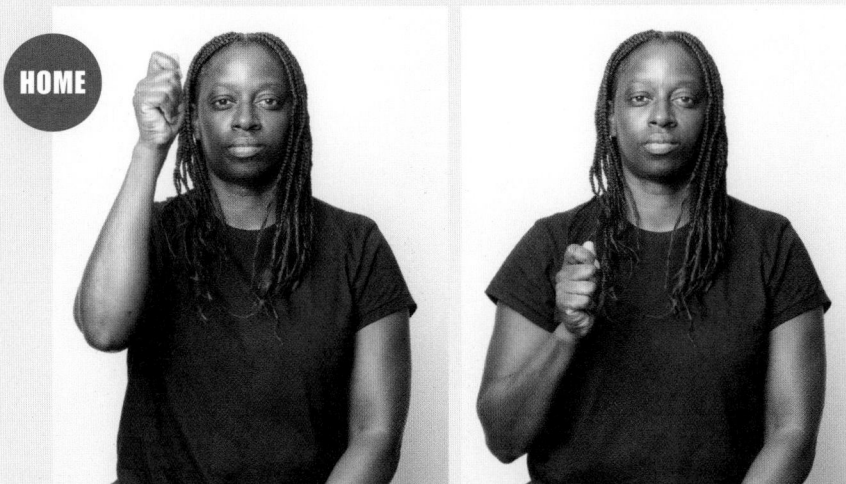

Place your right hand in a fist (A-handshape, page 22) with the hand turned so the thumb is on top. Place it above the side of the head and then move your arm vertically down.
Note: *The sign describes pulling the string for a light.*

HOW ARE YOU?

Place both hands flat, with the four fingers together and the thumb extended (flat B-handshape, page 22). With the palms facing you at chest level and the tips of the hands almost touching, open your hands in an arch toward the audience until the palms are facing up.
Note: *Make an inquisitive facial expression and head tilt.*

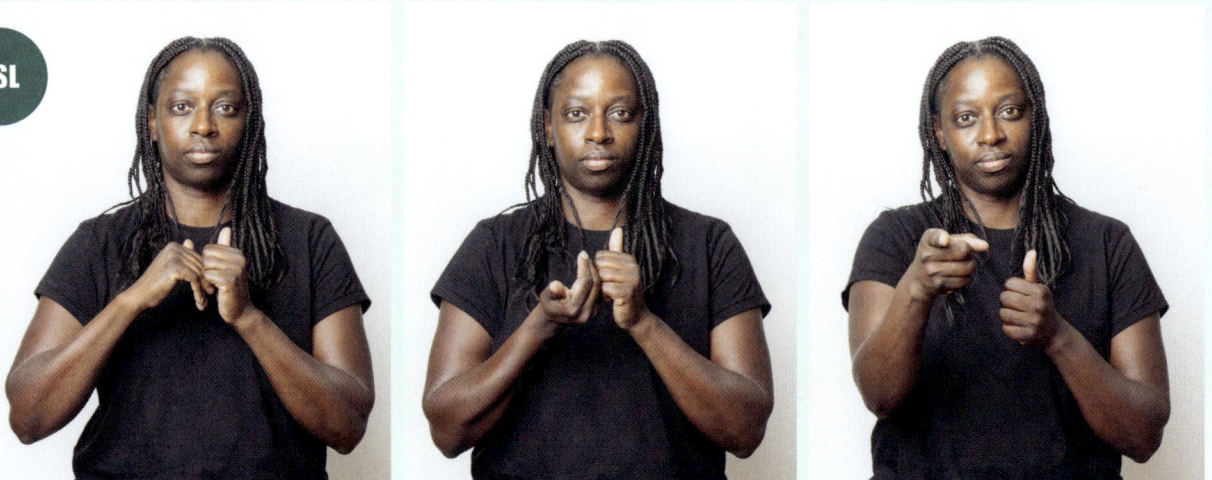

Place your hands curved, with the four fingers together and the thumb extended (A-handshape, page 22). With the palms facing down and the backs of the knuckles touching, move in a circular motion inward and up, then point with one index finger toward the audience.

THANK YOU

Place both hands flat, with the four fingers together and the thumb extended (flat B-handshape, page 22). Touch the fingertips to your chin, then move your hands forward.

Place your hand flat, with the four fingers together and the thumb extended (flat B-handshape, page 22). Touch the fingertips to your chin, then move your hand forward.

Franklin is signing the BASL Alabama variation of *pregnant* while Stephanie is signing the ASL variation (page 93).

BODY & HEALTH

DOCTOR

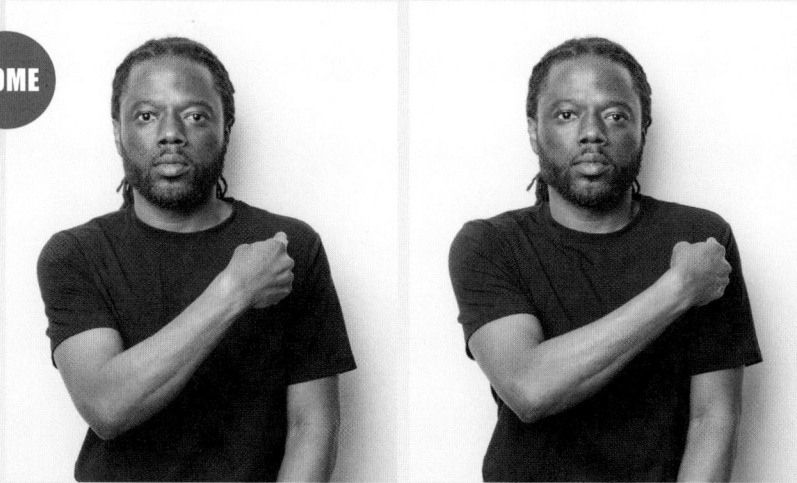

Place your right index finger on the shoulder of your left arm and tap twice.
Note: *The sign describes an injection shot in the arm.*

MEDICINE

Place your index finger and thumb together to make a circle, with the rest of the fingers curled into a fist. Then move your hand forward and back in front of your mouth.
Note: *The sign describes pills being put in the mouth.*

COUGH

Place your fist near your mouth and move both your head and fist forward repeatedly like you're coughing.

SICK

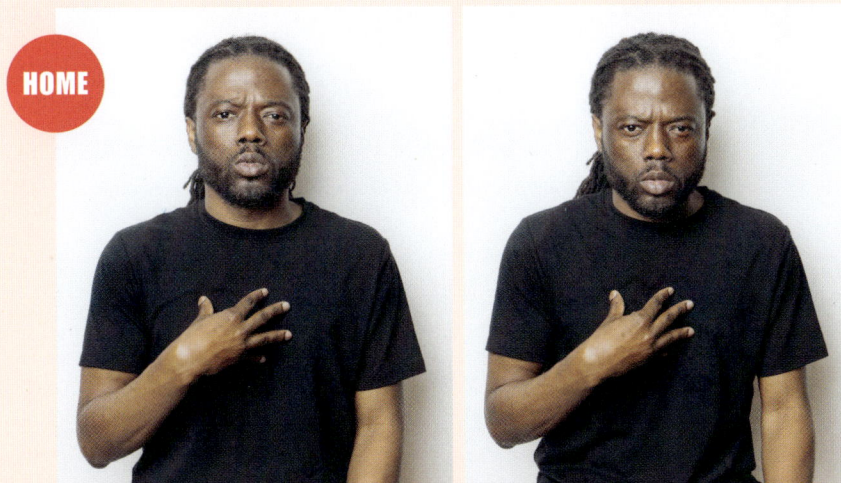

Place your hand in a scrunched 5-handshape, like you're squeezing something but your fingers are straight, over your chest. Shake it up and down with an intense mouth movement.
Note: *This sign can also indicate a cold as this means sickness in general.*

STOMACH UPSET

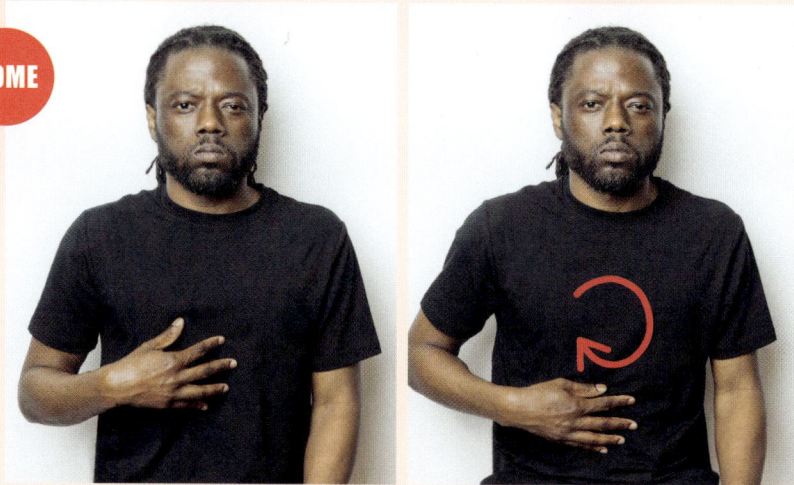

HOME

Place your hand in a 5-handshape on your stomach area and move it in a small circle.

FLU

HOME

Place your hand in a fist in front of your mouth. Then move both your hand and head back and forth with a "flu" mouth movement.

HEART

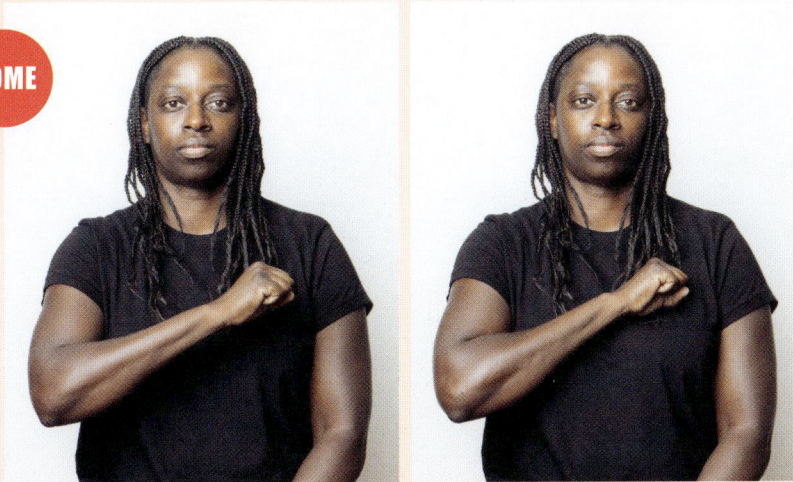

Place your hand in a fist, then tap the side of your fist over the heart area on the side of your chest twice.

Place your hand in a 5-handshape with your middle finger bent. Then position your hand on the side of your chest and tap twice.

FEVER

Place your hand flat, with the four fingers together and the thumb extended (flat B-handshape, page 22) with the palm facing the audience. Then tap your forehead with the back of your hand twice.

BALD

Place your hand flat, with the four fingers together and the thumb extended (flat B-handshape, page 22), and the palm down on the crown of your head. Move your hand in a circular motion.

PREGNANT ALABAMA

Extend the first two fingers of your hand with the fingers slightly spread (V-handshape, page 26). Start by pointing them at the bottom of your neck in the neutral space, then move toward the neck.

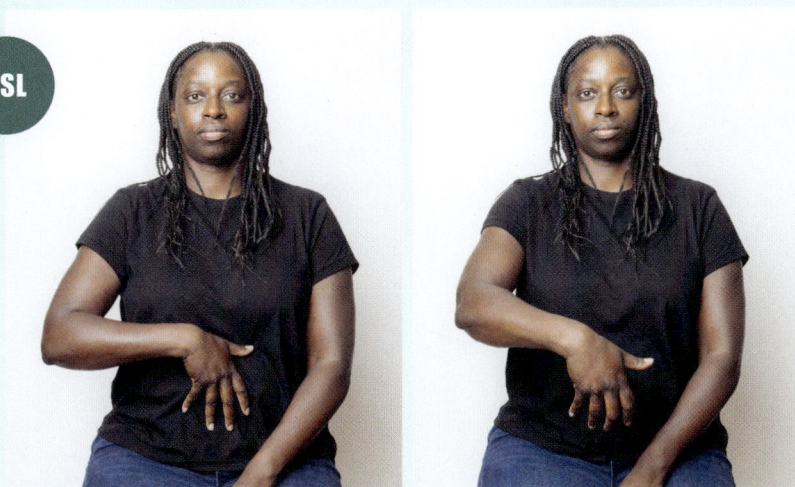

ASL

Place your hand in a curved 5-handshape on your stomach, with your fingertips pointing down. Then curve your hand while pulling your hand away from your body.

LONG HAIR

HOME

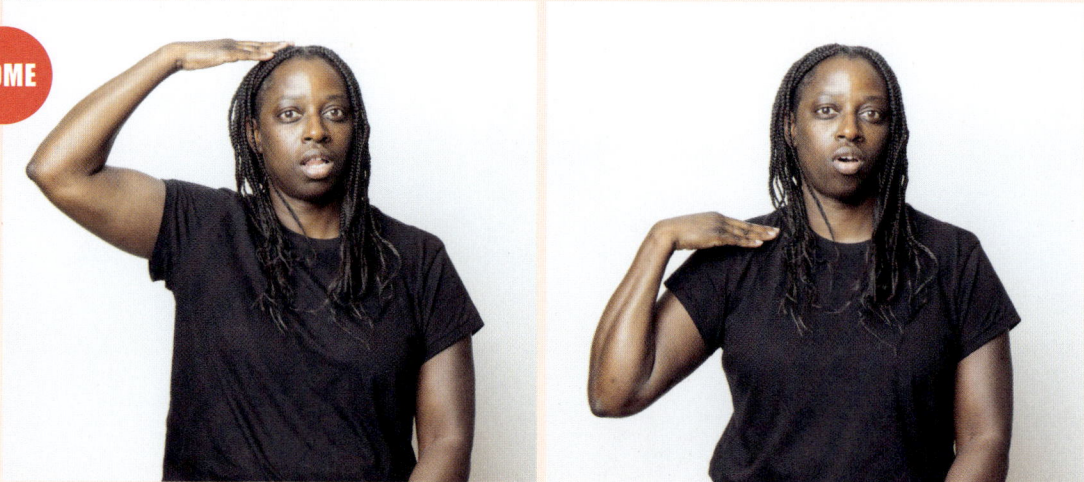

Place your hand flat (B-handshape, page 22) with your fingers touching the side of your head. Then drag your hand down to the shoulder. Make a "long hair" mouth movement.

SHORT HAIR

HOME

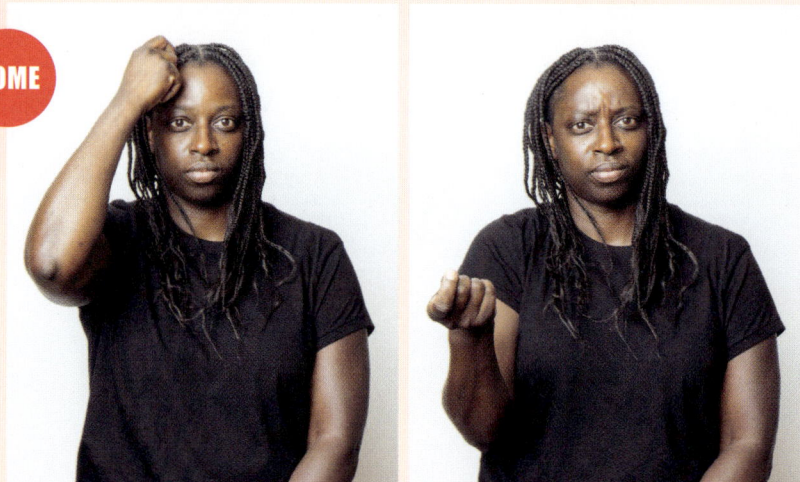

Touch your index finger and thumb together to make a circle, with the rest of the fingers curled into a fist. Then touch the top of your head and move your hand forward in an arc to the neutral space.

Franklin is signing the word *shark* (page 102) while Stephanie is signing the Home sign for *fish* (page 103).

ANIMALS

CAT

Place your left hand in a curved 5-handshape, with the four fingers together and the thumb extended (B-handshape, page 22). Make the right hand into a claw shape and touch the fingertips to the left palm. Open and close your right fingers while pulling away from the left hand to mimic scratching.

BIG CAT

Place your hands curved and move them in front of you in large, downward scratching motions, like a lion.
Note: The sign is the same for lion, tiger, and other big cats.

DOG

Place your hand at chin level. Point your thumb, index, and middle fingers toward the audience, with the ring and pinky curled. Touch the top of your wrist to your chin twice.

Place your hand in the neutral space with the palm facing up. With your middle finger and thumb, snap your fingers twice.

BIRD

Place both hands in a horizontal 5-handshape at shoulder level. Then flap your hands up and down, imitating a bird's wings.

HORSE

Place your hands on top of your head and point both index fingers back so the palms are facing up. Flick your hands forward twice in a quick movement.
Note: The motion mimics the way a horse's ears move.

GOAT

HOME

Hold your hands on top of your head, with the index fingers curled like a hook (X-handshape, page 26) and the palms facing away from the audience.
Note: Your fingers should mimic goat horns.

DEER

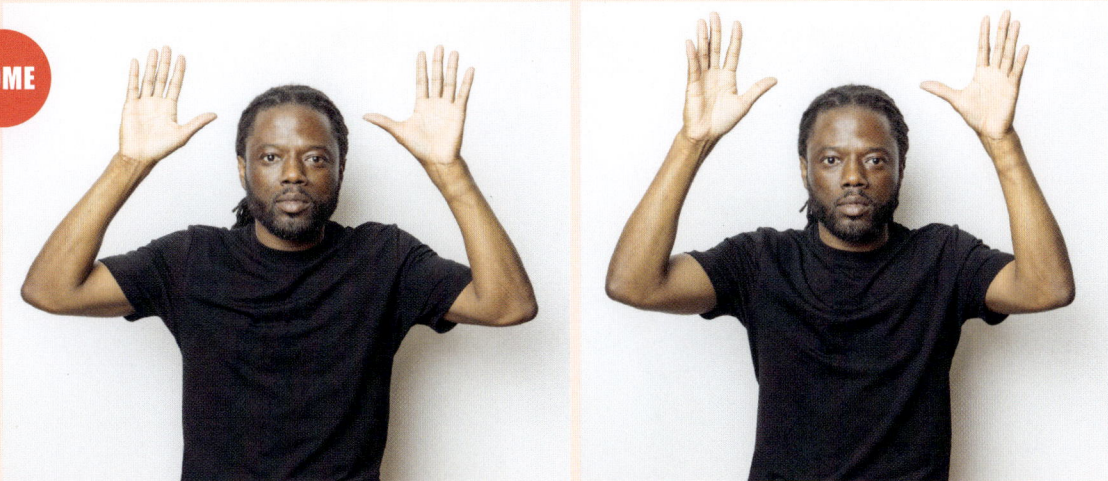

HOME

Place both hands into a 5-handshape above your head with the palms facing slightly up, then move them forward twice.

RACCOON

Place both index and middle fingers split around your eyes. Then pull your hands out to the sides twice.

SHARK

HOME

Place your left arm extended with your left index finger pointing toward the audience. Make a fist with your right hand, then drag the fist from the tip of the left finger down the arm.
Note: The sign describes how to remove the skin of a shark.

FISH

Point your left index finger up. Then swipe the back of your right index finger against the side of the left index finger twice.
Note: *The sign looks as if you are scaling the fish.*

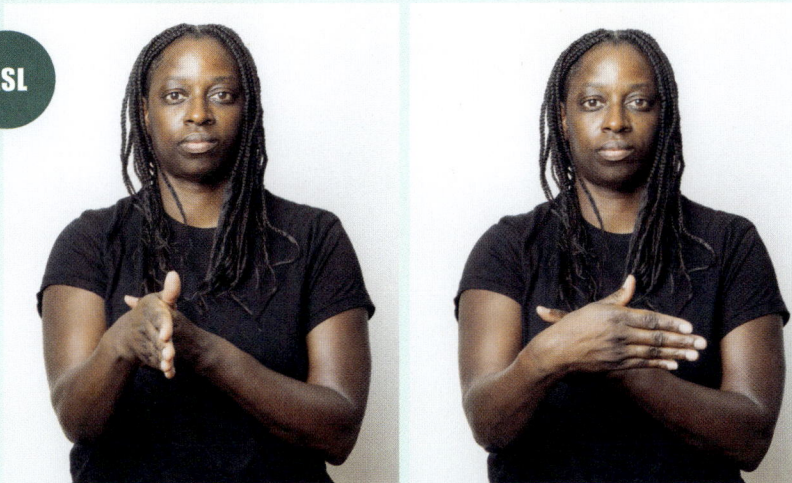

Place both hands in a 5-handshape with thumbs slightly tucked into the palms. With your right palm facing the left, place the tips of your left hand against the base of your right palm. Then flap the right hand against the back of the left hand as if your hand is a fish swimming in the water.

FROG

Place your hands at chest level and point the index fingers out to the sides. Then make a circle with both hands, moving outward and then meeting in the middle.

LIZARD

Hold your hand in front of your mouth. Point the thumb, index, and middle fingers at the audience, with your thumb underneath the two other fingers.
Note: The sign looks like the forked tongue of some lizards.

SNAKE

Point your index finger out to the side, then move your hand in a winding path in the neutral space toward the audience.
Note: *The sign describes how a snake moves.*

BEE

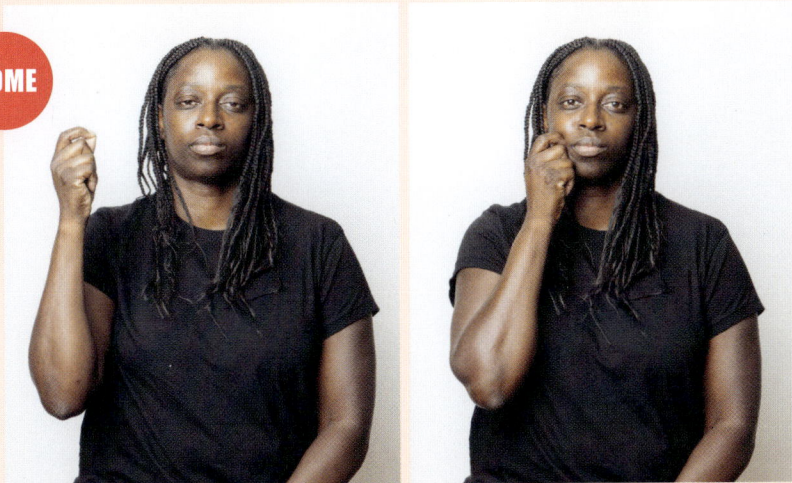

Place the index finger and thumb together and keep the rest of the fingers curled. Then tap your cheek twice.
Note: *The sign looks like a bee is stinging your cheek.*

Franklin is signing the word *tea* (page 128) while Stephanie is signing the BASL Virginia variation of the word *cheese* (page 115).

FOOD & DRINK

FOOD

HOME

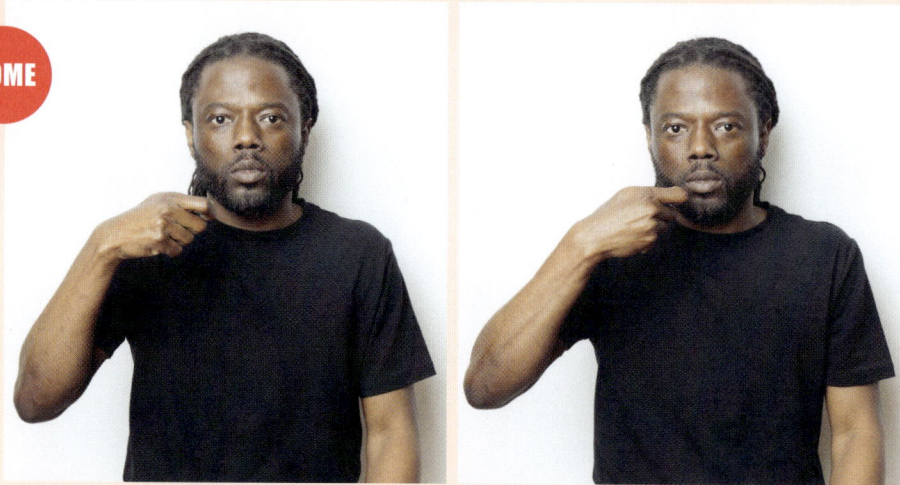

Place your index finger and thumb together, with the rest of the fingers curled. Then make scooping motions with your hand close to the mouth with a "food" mouth movement.

PEACH NORTH CAROLINA

Place both hands in a 5-handshape, with the left hand in front of you in the neutral space and your right hand in a bent 5-handshape that hovers over the left. Close and open your right hand twice while touching your left hand.
Note: *The sign looks like you are "picking" a peach.*

PEACH TEXAS

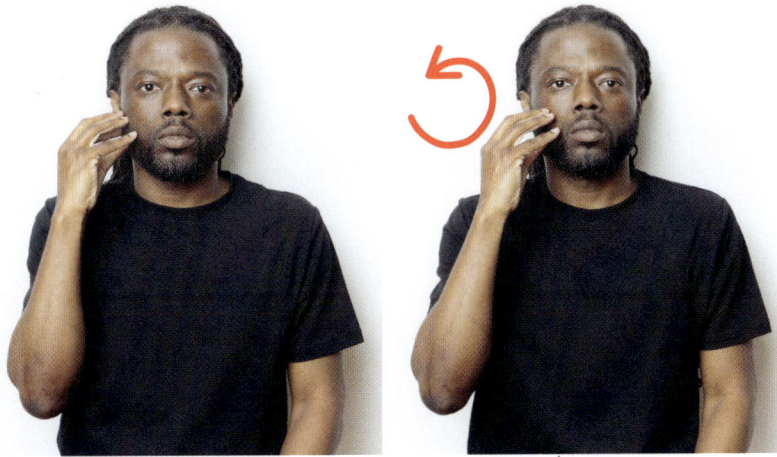

Place your right hand in a claw handshape on the right side of the cheek and make a clockwise movement twice.

WATERMELON

HOME

Place both hands flat, with the four fingers together and the thumb extended (flat B-handshape, page 22). Then hold the left hand palm up and move the side of the right hand down your left palm in a slicing motion.

APPLE

HOME

Place your hand in a curved 5-handshape (C-handshape, page 22) near the mouth with the palm up. Then move it upward twice.

ASL

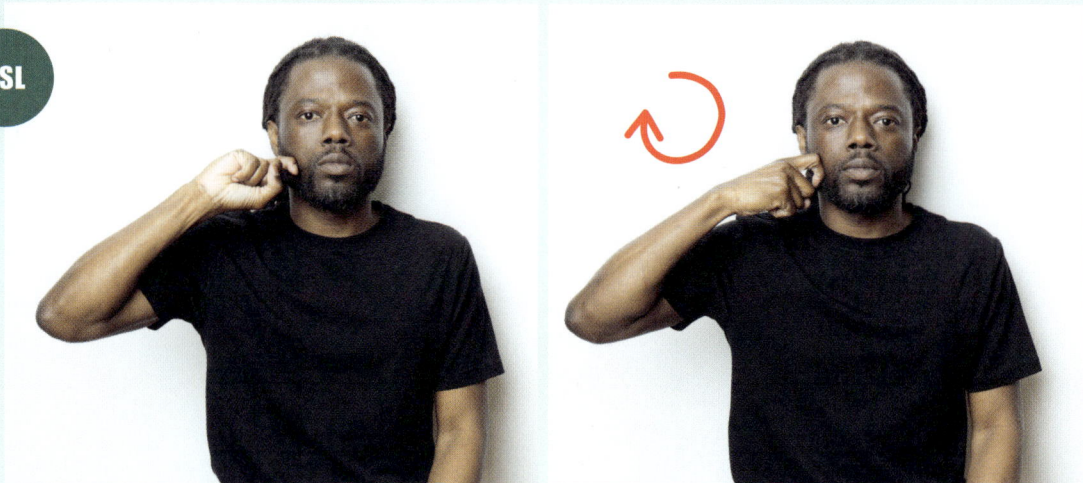

Place your index finger in a hook with the rest of the fingers and thumb curled into a fist (X-handshape, page 26) against your cheek and twist it forward twice.

LEMON NORTH CAROLINA

Place your index finger to your lips and tap twice.

LEMON TEXAS

Place your hand into a fist near your mouth, then slightly open and close your fist twice like you're squeezing a lemon.

ONION

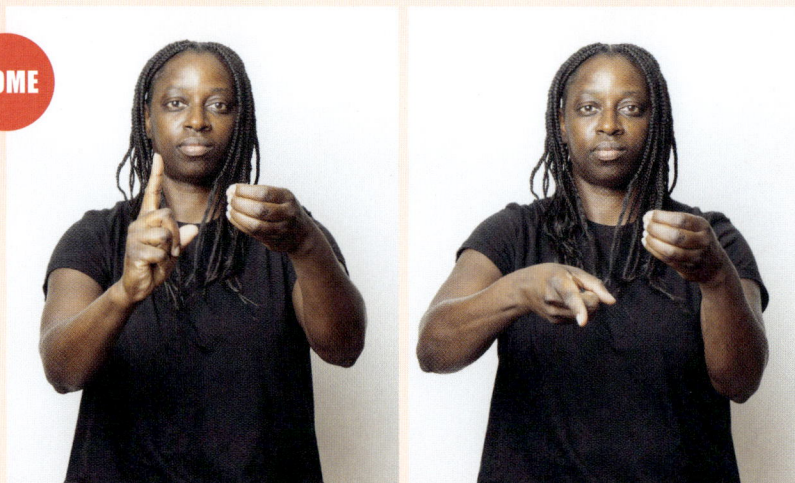

Touch all five fingers of your left hand together (O-handshape, page 24). Point the right index finger and swipe it against the tips of the left hand fingers twice.

CARROT

Place your hands above the sides of your head and point your index fingers up. Rotate your hands forward and back twice. Then, place the left index finger in the neutral space pointing forward and let the right index finger make contact and swipe toward you twice.

CABBAGE

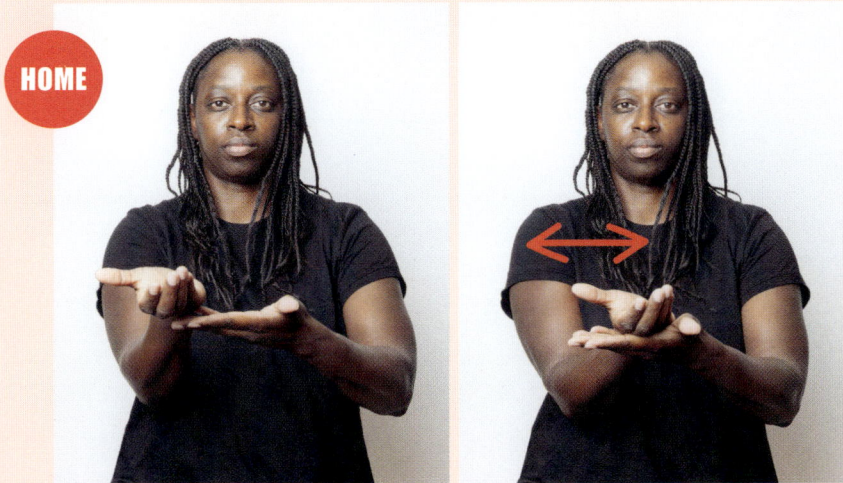

Place both hands in a curved 5-handshape with the palms facing up. Position your left hand at chest level and brush the back of your right hand against your left palm twice.
Note: *The sign looks like you are cutting a head of cabbage.*

COLLARD

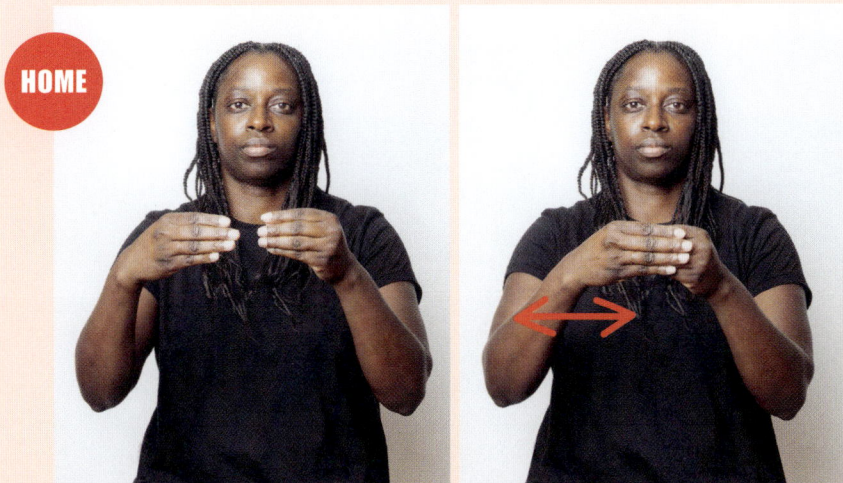

Touch all five fingers of the left hand together (O-handshape, page 24) and curve the right hand (closed C-handshape, page 22). Then cover your left hand with your right and pull back to the right twice. As you move, close the fingers of your right hand together.
Note: *The sign describes how to remove the collards from the stem.*

OKRA

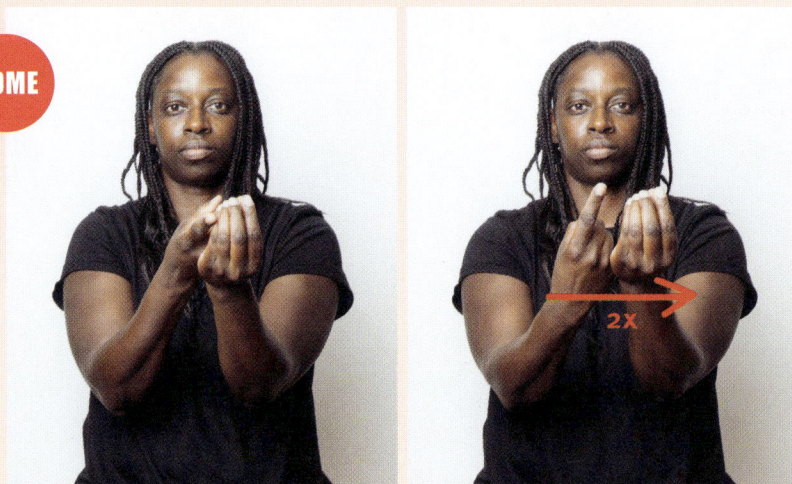

Touch all five fingers of the left hand together (O-handshape, page 24). Keep the left hand still with the fingers pointing up, then point the right index finger and swipe it twice over the tips of the left fingers.

Note: *The sign describes how to cut the head of okra.*

POTATO VIRGINIA

Place your right hand flat, with the four fingers together and the thumb extended (flat B-handshape, page 22) and touch your mouth. Then place your left hand flat. Flip your right hand so the wrist touches your left hand, then tap the back of your left hand.

CHEESE VIRGINIA

Place your index and middle fingers bent with the rest of your fingers curled together (bent V-handshape, page 26) on your face. First touch the middle of your forehead and then your chin.

EGG

HOME

Place your index finger and thumb together to make an oval shape over your right eye. The index finger and thumb should not be touching.

CHICKEN TEXAS

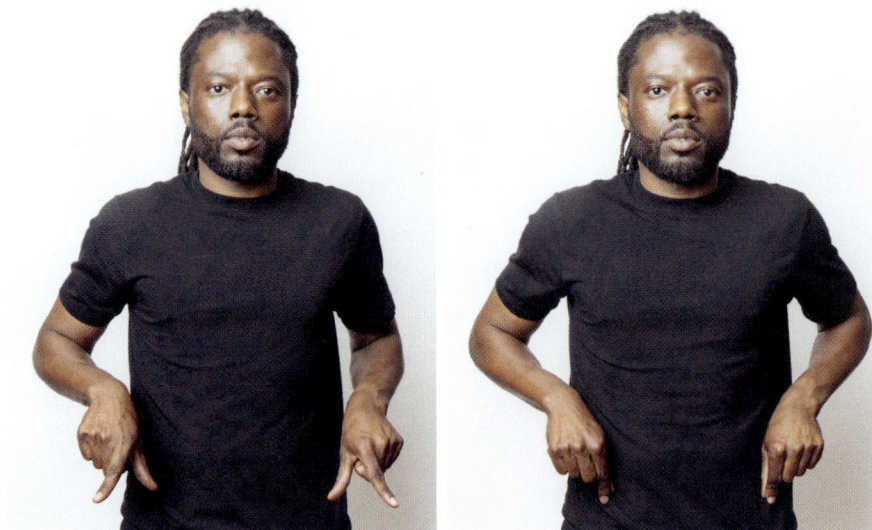

Extend your thumb and index fingers, with the rest of the fingers curled together (open F-handshape, page 23). Point your fingers down at the side of your waist and tap them together.

HAM

HOME

Place your left hand in a fist and your right hand in a 5-handshape. Then slide the right palm against the side of your left fist.
Note: The sign describes how to cut a slice of ham.

SHRIMP

HOME

Place both hands in fists with the knuckles of your index fingers slightly raised. Then move both thumbs against the index fingers twice.
Note: *The sign describes how to pinch the head off a shrimp.*

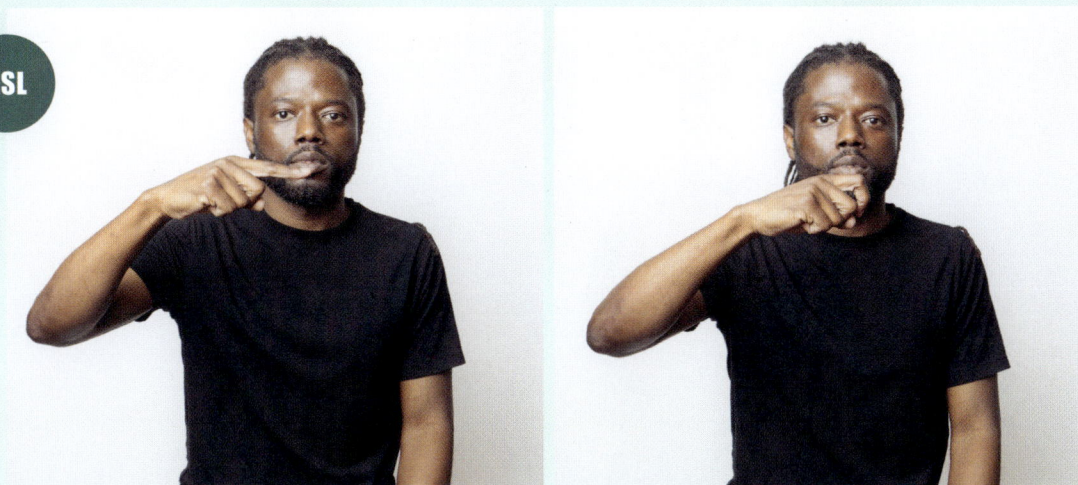

ASL

Place the index finger straight, then bend it (X-handshape, page 26) while moving twice horizontally in the neutral space.

FLOUNDER

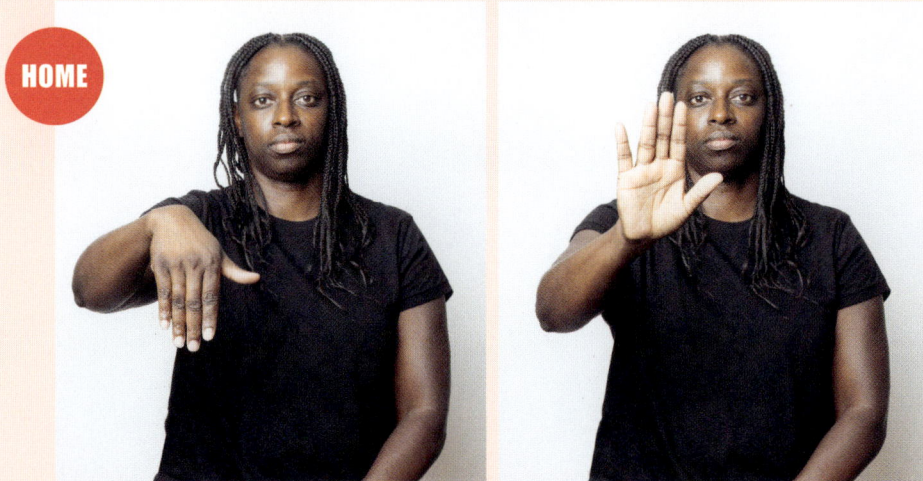

Place your hand in the neutral space with the palm facing the audience. Then make your hand flap up and down in the air, like a fish's tail.
Note: *The sign describes how a flounder moves.*

OYSTER

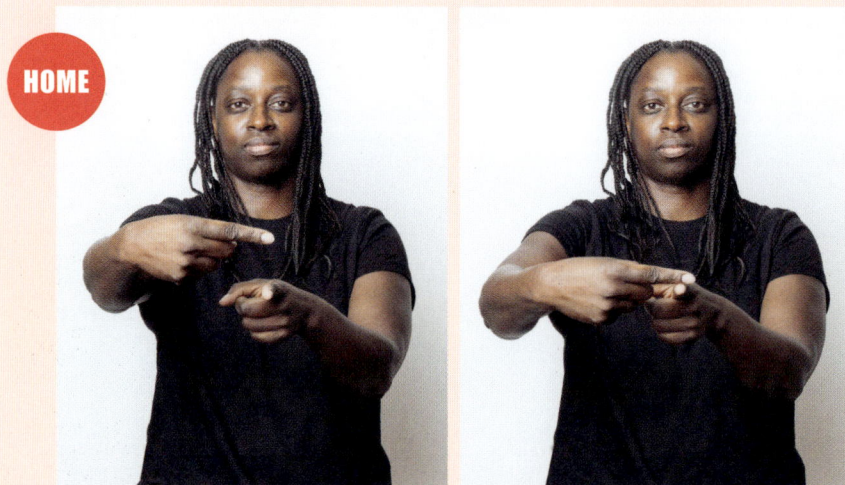

Place both hands in a fist with the index fingers pointed. Then tap the right index finger against the left index finger twice.
Note: *The sign shows the action of cracking open an oyster.*

CONCH

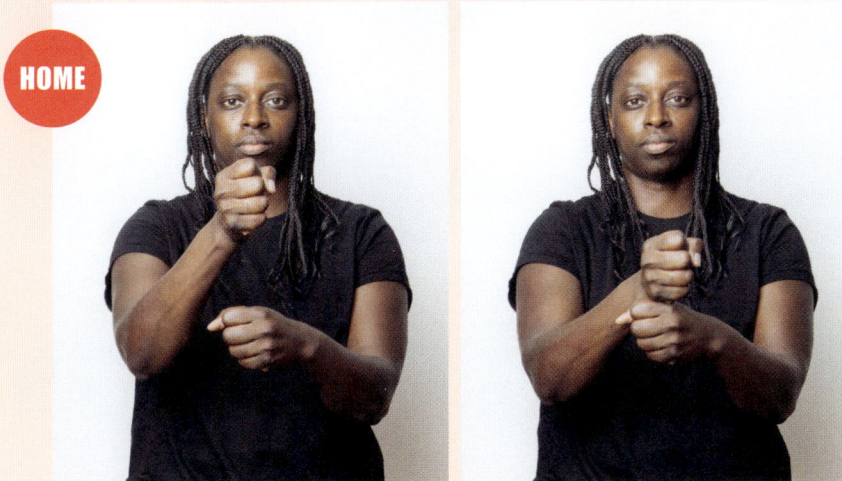

Place your left hand in a fist and hold it in the neutral space. With your right hand also in a fist, tap the side of the left fist and drag it back toward yourself.

RICE

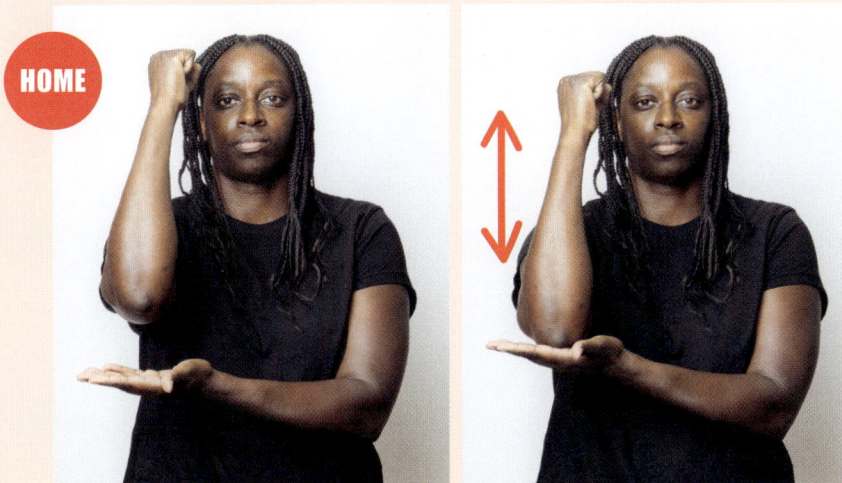

Place your hand flat, with the four fingers together and the thumb extended (flat B-handshape, page 22) and position it under your right elbow. Then tap your right elbow up and down twice in the palm of your left hand.

BREAD

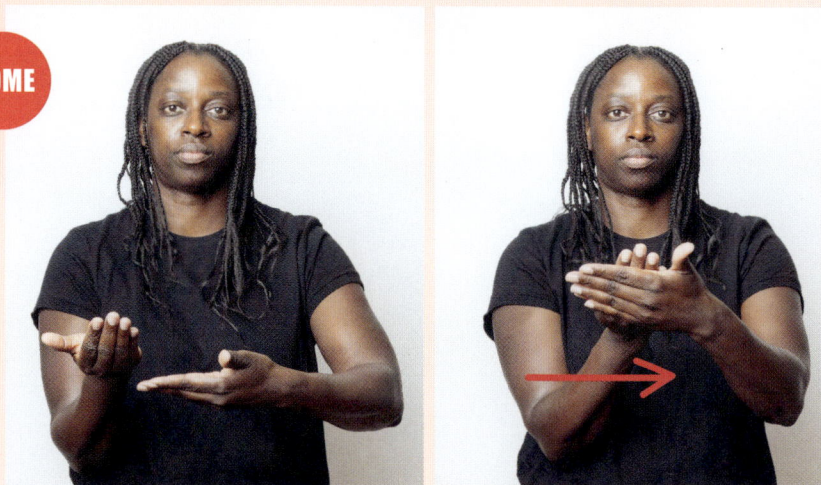

Place both hands palm up, then sweep the back of your right hand over the palm of your left in two quick movements.

CRACKER VIRGINIA

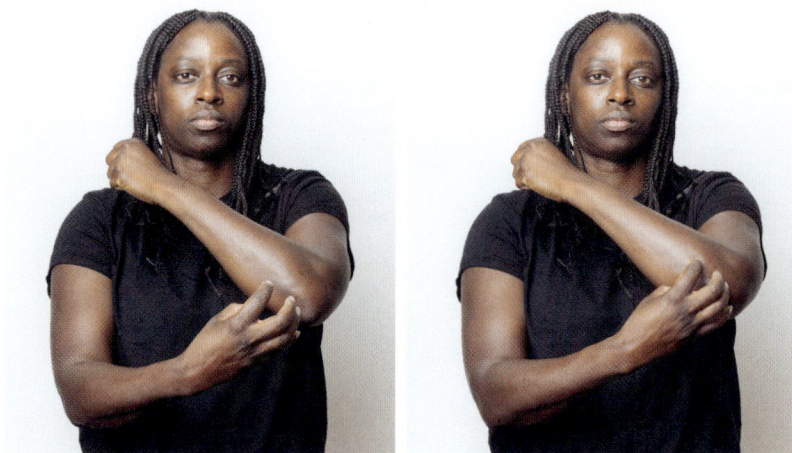

Place your left arm horizontal while your right hand, in a bent 5-handshape, taps the left elbow twice.

OATMEAL

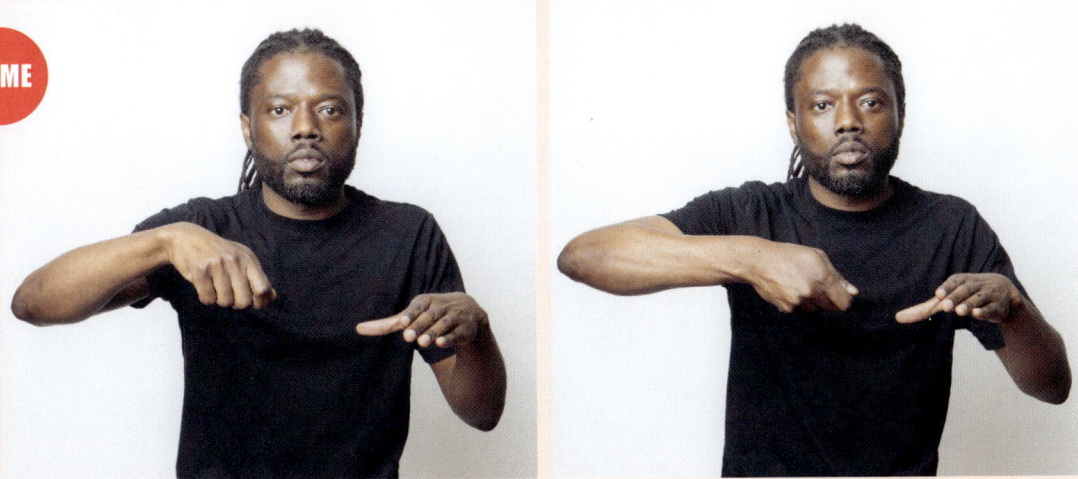

HOME

Place your right index finger and thumb together while the rest of the fingers are closed. Place the left hand curved (C-handshape, page 22) and move your right hand in a circular motion in the space between the left fingers and thumb, like you're mixing. Then move the right hand to the side of your mouth and tap twice, making a mouth movement for "oatmeal."

BISCUIT

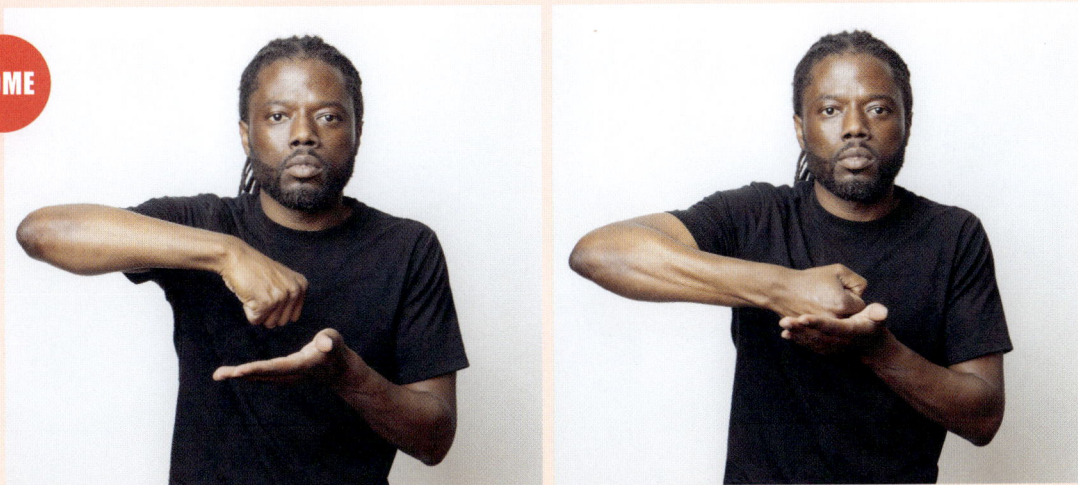

HOME

Place the left hand in a curved 5-handshape, with the four fingers together and the thumb extended (flat B-handshape, page 22). Place the right hand in a fist, then push the fist into your left hand and twist.
Note: The sign describes how to knead biscuit dough.

GRAVY

HOME

Place both hands flat, with the four fingers together and the thumb extended (flat B-handshape, page 22). Touch the back of the right hand to the palm of the left hand and move it in a circular motion.

CEREAL

HOME

Place your right index finger and thumb together while the rest of the fingers are closed and move your hand down the center of your chest twice. Then tap your right elbow into your left palm twice.

PANCAKE

HOME

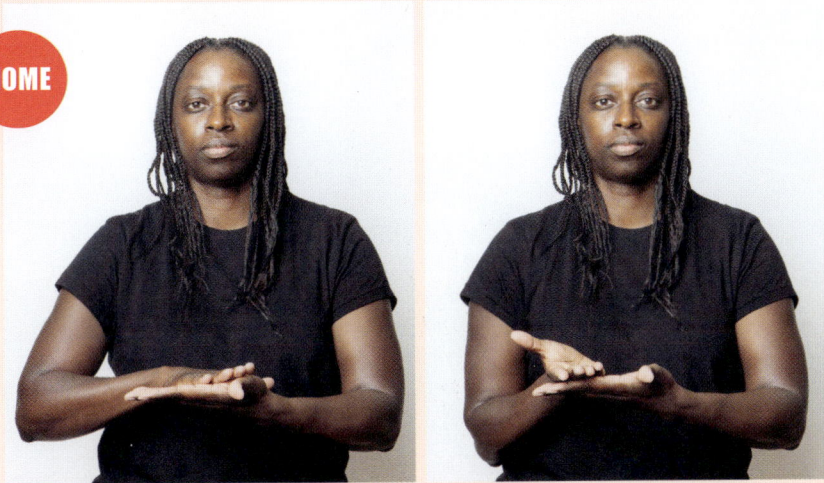

Place your right hand flat, with the four fingers together and the thumb extended
(flat B-handshape, page 22), with the palm facing down above the palm of your left hand.
Flip your right palm up and down in your left hand twice.
Note: The sign mimics flipping a pancake.

PEANUT TEXAS

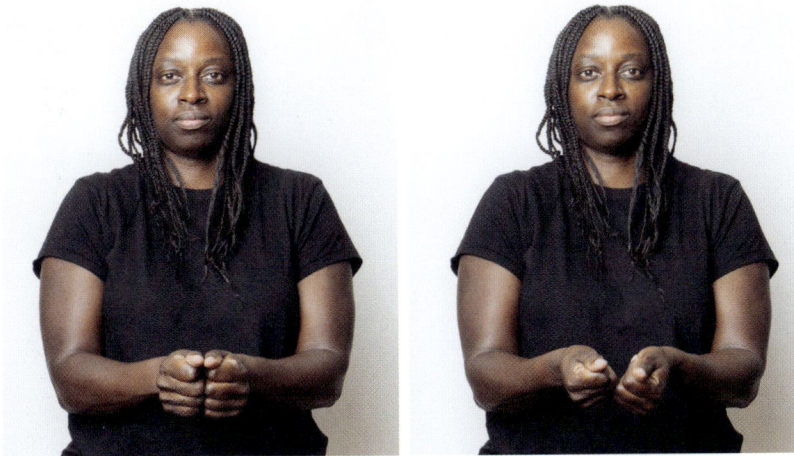

Place your hands in fists with the knuckles touching. Then rotate your hands in opposite
directions twice.

PECAN

HOME

Touch the index finger and thumb together, with the rest of the fingers curled (bent G-handshape, page 23), and place it in the corner of your mouth. Move your jaw like you're biting.
Note: *The sign shows the action of trying to crack a pecan in your mouth.*

PIE NORTH CAROLINA

Place your left hand flat with the fingertips pointing up, then bend your right fingers in a 90-degree angle. Touch the right fingers to the left palm and twist the right hand forward twice.

CAKE NORTH CAROLINA

Place your hand in a 5-handshape and touch your mouth. Then brush your fingertips downward against your mouth.

CAKE VIRGINIA

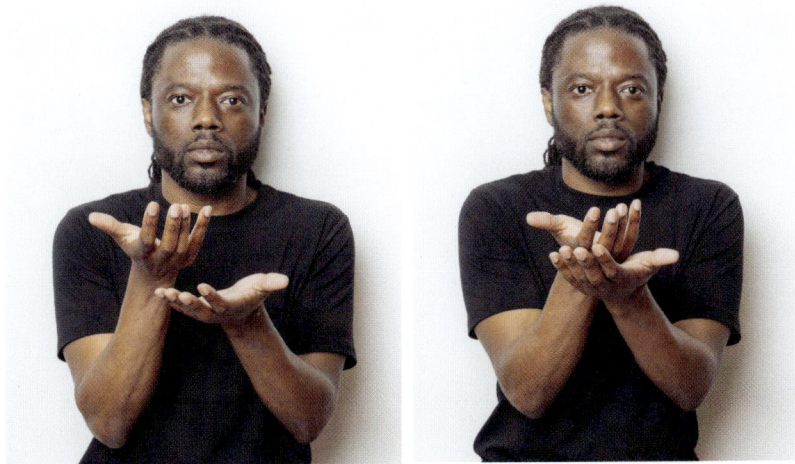

Place your left hand in front of you at about chest level with the palm facing up. Then hit the back of your right hand against the palm of your left hand twice.

CANDY

Place your index finger across your lips, where your top and bottom lips meet. Then slide your finger horizontally.

Place your index finger pointed at the side of your cheek. Then twist your finger twice.

WATER VIRGINIA

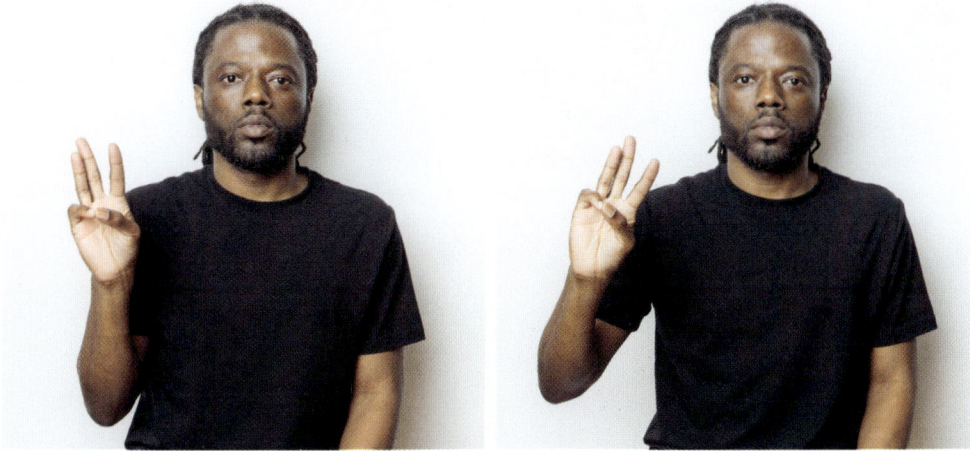

Extend and spread the first three fingers (W-handshape, page 26). Then shake your hand from side to side.

Extend and spread the first three fingers (W-handshape, page 26), then use the side of your index finger to tap the middle of the chin twice.

MILK

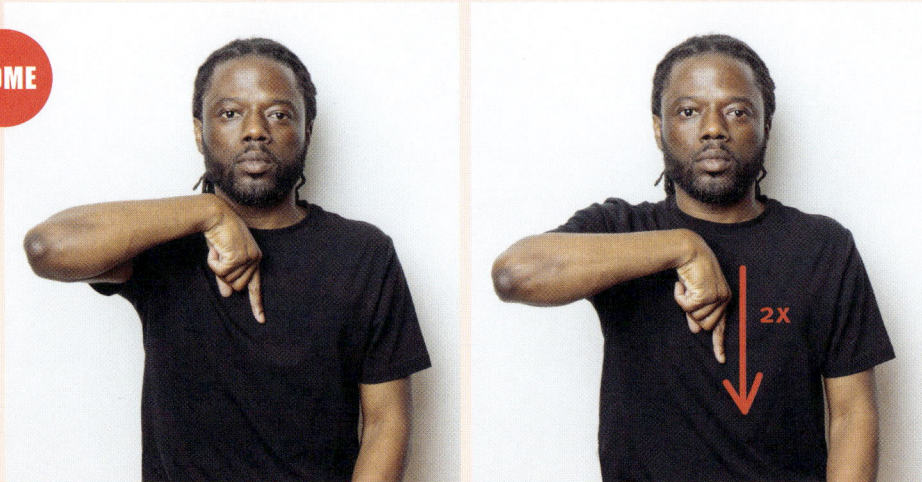

Point your index finger down in the middle of your chest, then move it up and down twice.

TEA

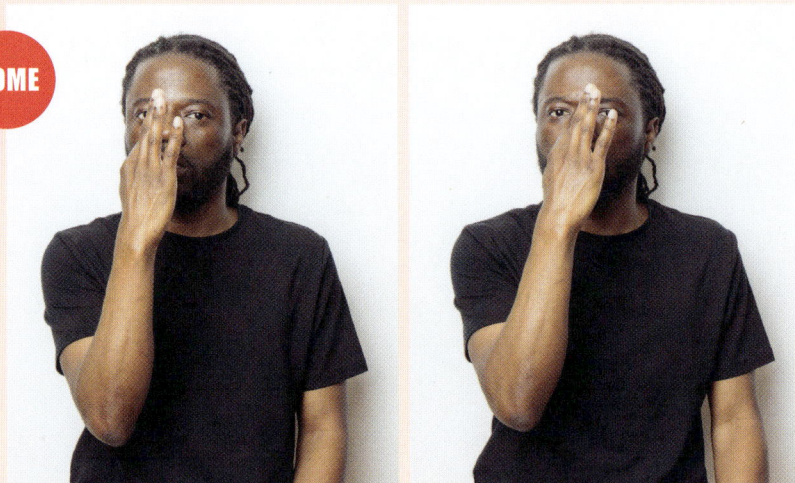

Place your thumb and index finger together, then tap your teeth twice.

WINE

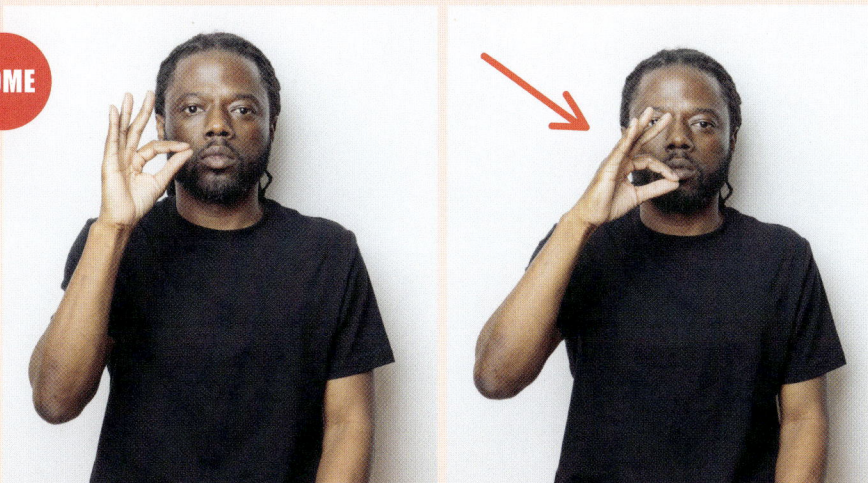

Place your index finger and thumb together while the other fingers are extended (F-handshape, page 22) at the upper side of your cheek. Then move your hand down in a diagonal, past your chin to the neutral space.

COFFEE

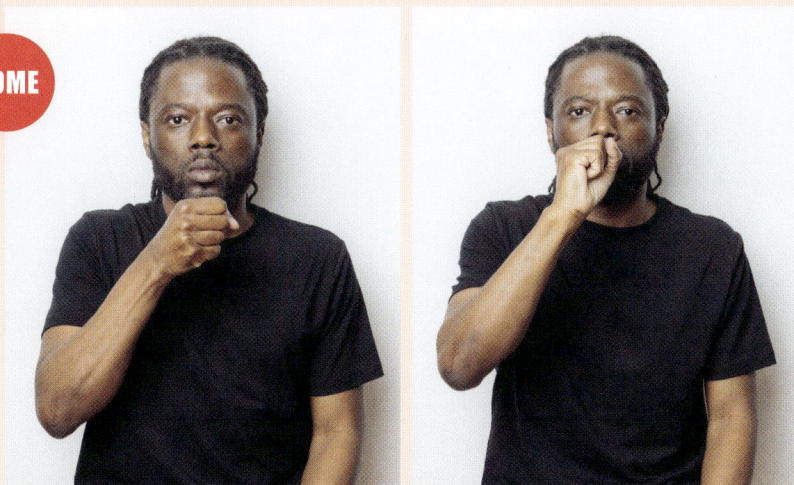

Place your fist in front of your mouth, then tilt your hand toward your mouth twice.
Note: *The sign describes the motion of drinking from a coffee mug.*

Franklin is signing the BASL Texas variation for the word *see*
while Stephanie is signing the ASL variation (page 135).

VERBS

EAT

HOME

Place your fist at chest level, with your thumb and index finger pinched together. Then move it toward your mouth with a quick, repetitive twisting movement.
Note: This motion looks as if you are using a utensil to bring food to your mouth.

GO CRABBING

HOME

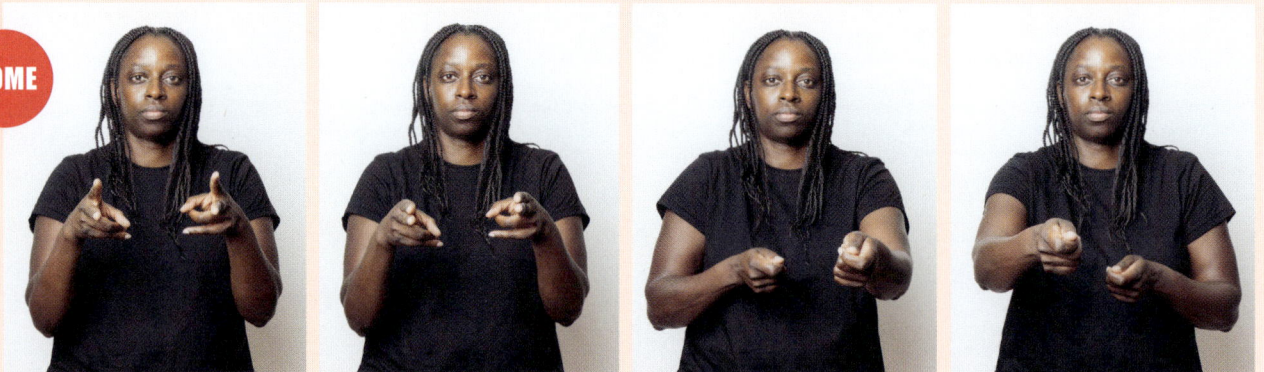

Point the index and middle fingers (V-handshape, page 26) and close them like scissors. Then close your hands into fists, with your thumb and index fingers pinched together. Pull your hands toward you, one after the other, like pulling a string.

FRY

HOME

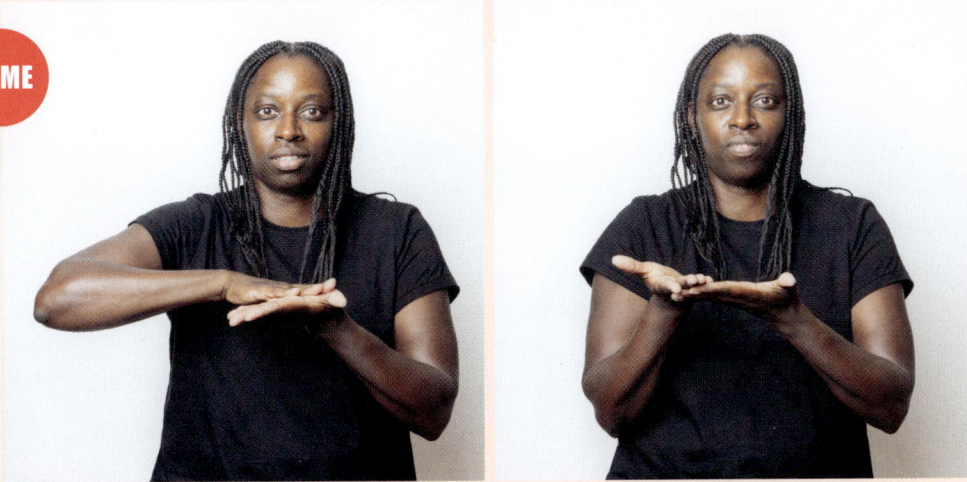

Place your left hand flat, with the palm facing up in the neutral space. With your right hand, keep it flat and flip the palm back and forth on top of your left palm, repeating the motion twice.

BOIL

HOME

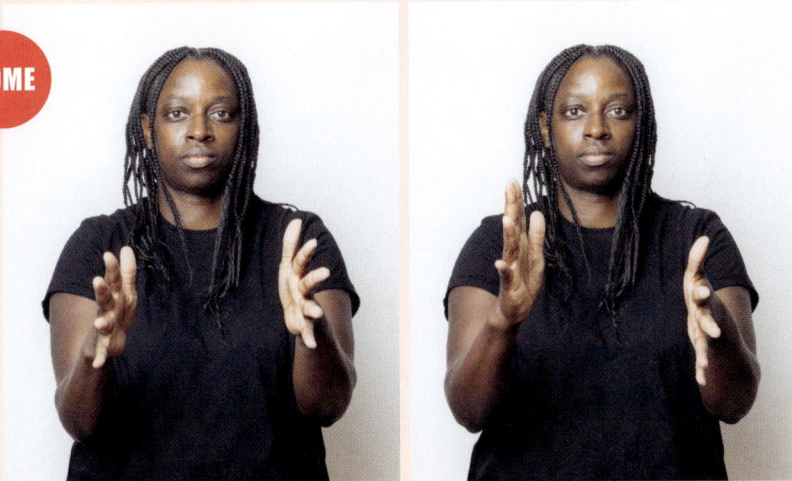

Make both hands a 5-handshape. With the palms facing each other, rotate your hands in opposite directions.

CLEAN NORTH CAROLINA

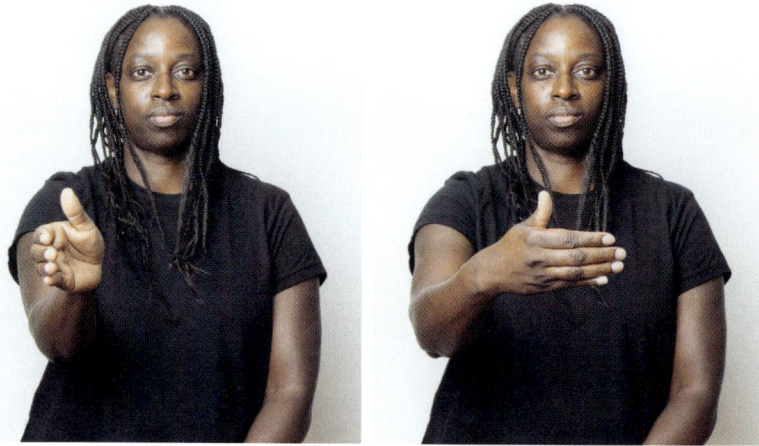

Loosely bend and unbend the fingers of your hand toward your chest, using quick movements.

SIT

HOME

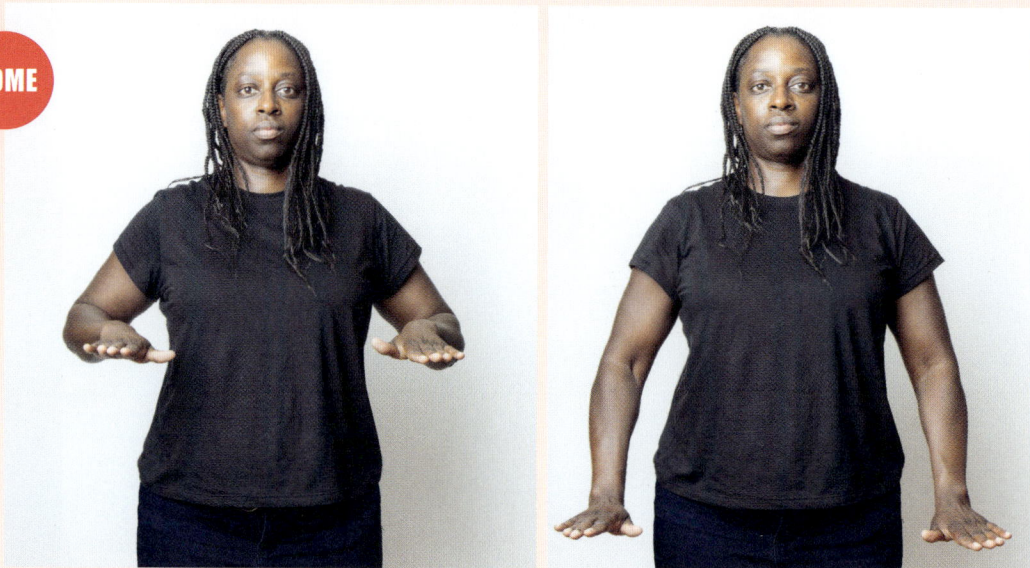

Place your hands out in front of you at chest level, with the palms facing down. Then push your hands down vertically.

SEE TEXAS

Bend your index and middle fingers in a hook, with the rest of the fingers closed, then tap the chin twice.

Extend your two first fingers (bent V-handshape, page 26) with the palm facing you. Place your hand just under your eyes, then move it forward, toward the audience in the neutral space.

SLEEP

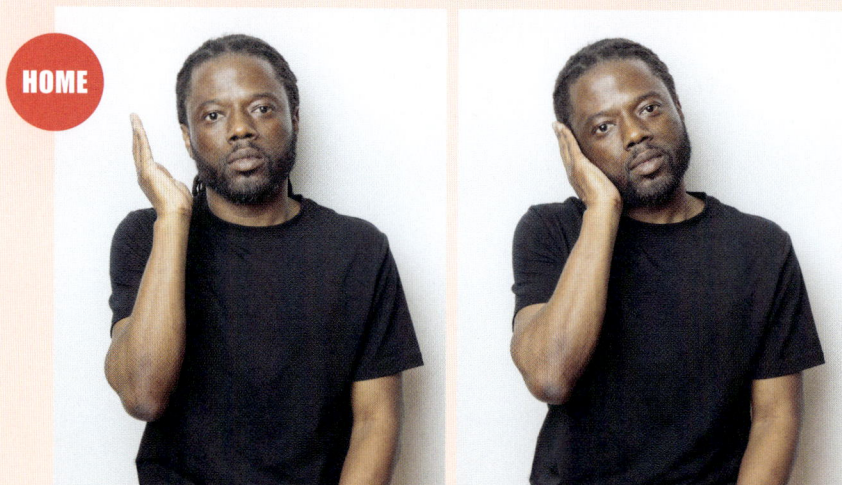

Place your hand in a slightly curved 5-handshape near your cheek. Then tilt your head until your palm is against the side of your head.

THINK

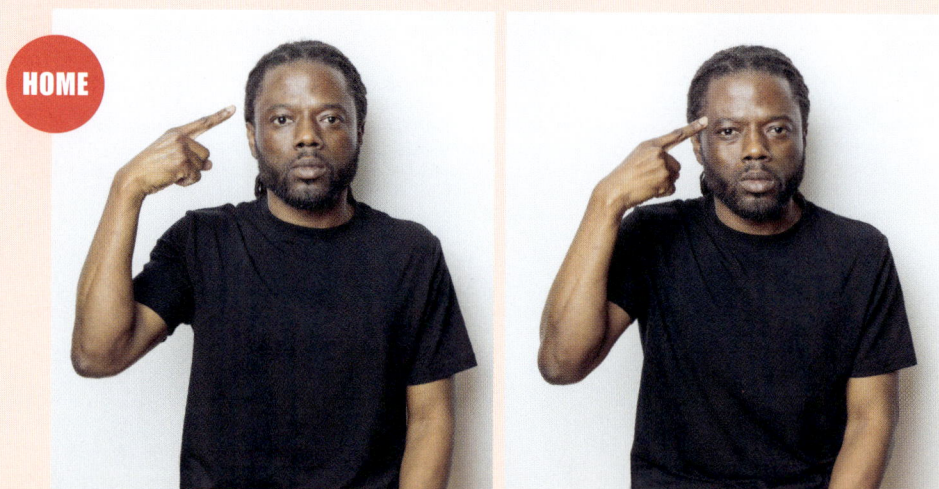

Point your index finger. Starting in the neutral space, move your hand to touch the side of your head. Make a "thinking" facial expression.

KNOW

Point your index finger. Starting in the neutral space, move your hand to the side of your head near the ear, and nod your head.

I DON'T KNOW

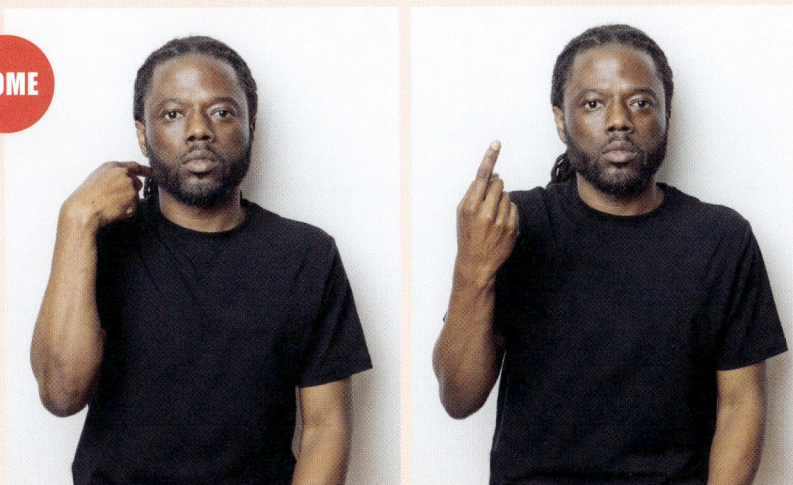

Point your index finger and touch the back of your finger to the side of your ear. Then move in an arc toward the neutral space, ending with your palm up.
Note: *Make sure to shake your head while signing.*

WORRY

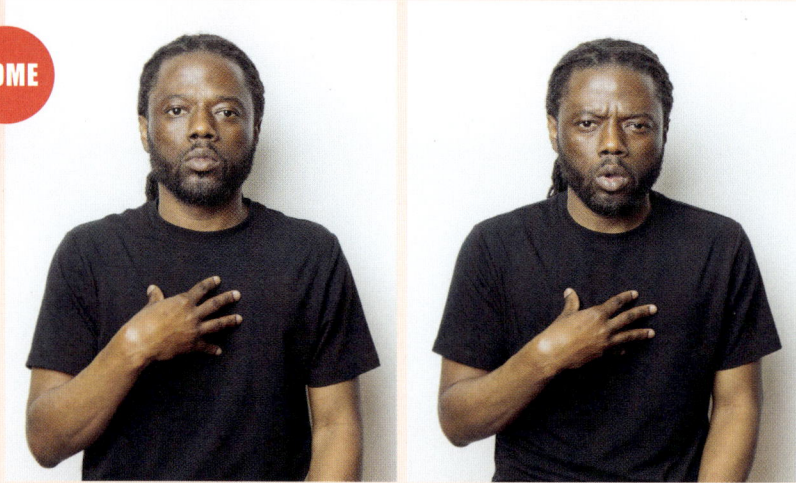

Place your hand in a 5-handshape with the fingers slightly curved on your chest and tilt your head forward while making the mouth movement for "worry."

FORGET

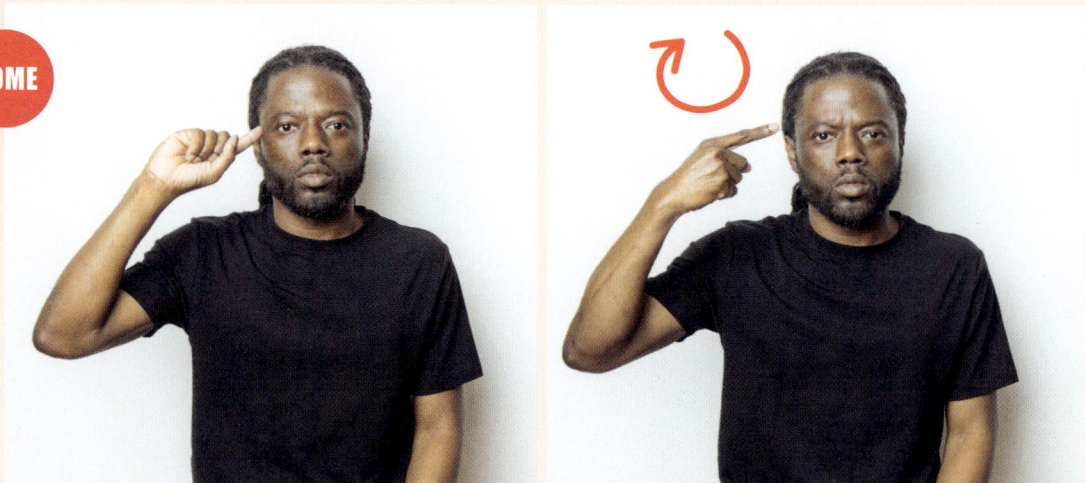

Point your index finger at the side of your head. Then twist your hand clockwise, so that the back of the hand is now facing the audience.

TELL

HOME

Point your index finger and keep your thumb extended. Then touch the middle of the chin with the back of your index finger and move it toward the audience.

CALL

HOME

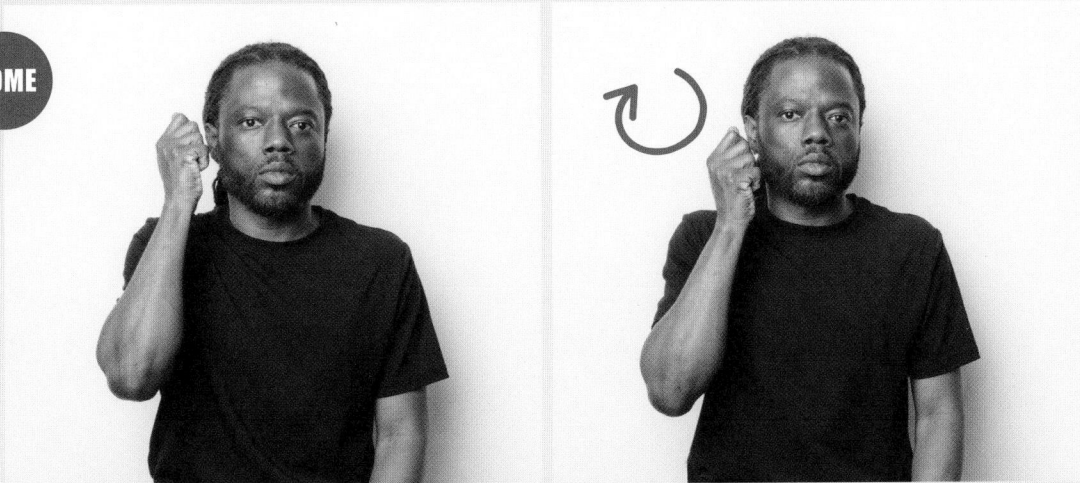

Place your hand in a fist by your ear, then move your hand clockwise in a circle twice.

GO

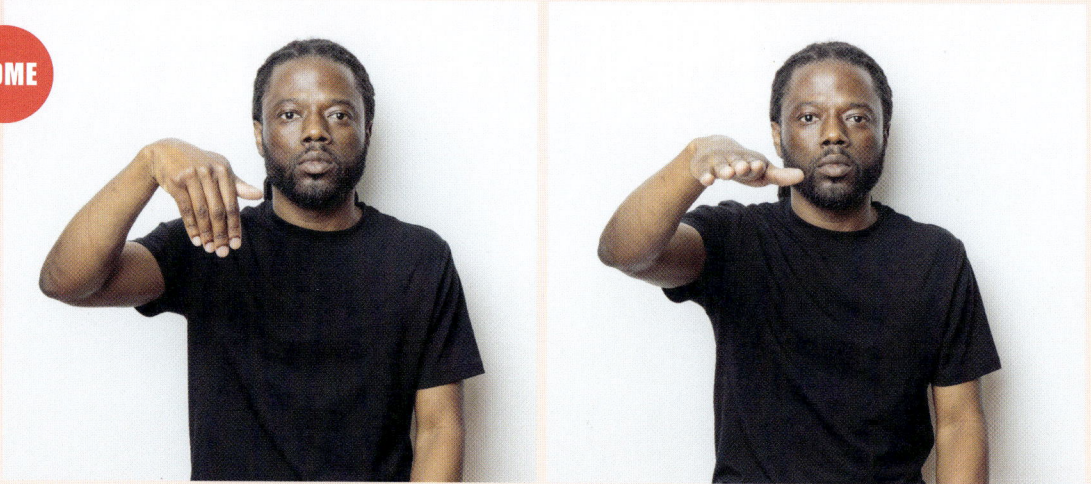

Place your hand bent at the wrist at chest level, then sweep it up and out until the hand is flat.
Note: This sign is the same for leave.

COME

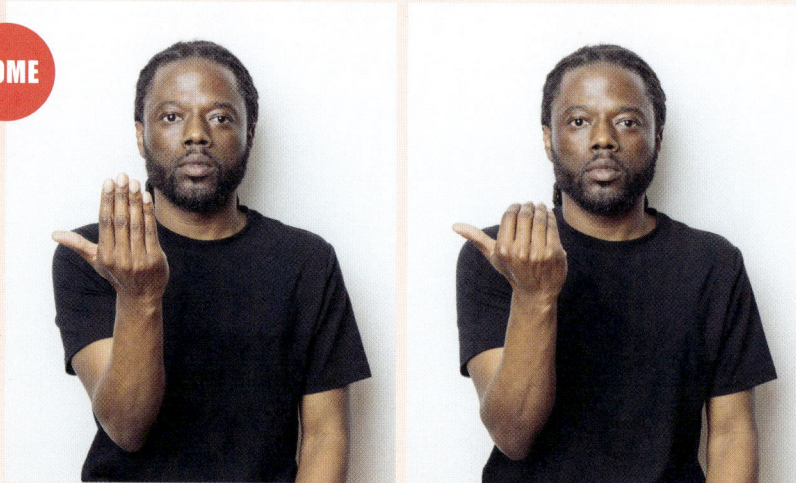

Place your curved hand, palm facing up, at chest level in the neutral space, then motion the audience toward you.

COME BACK

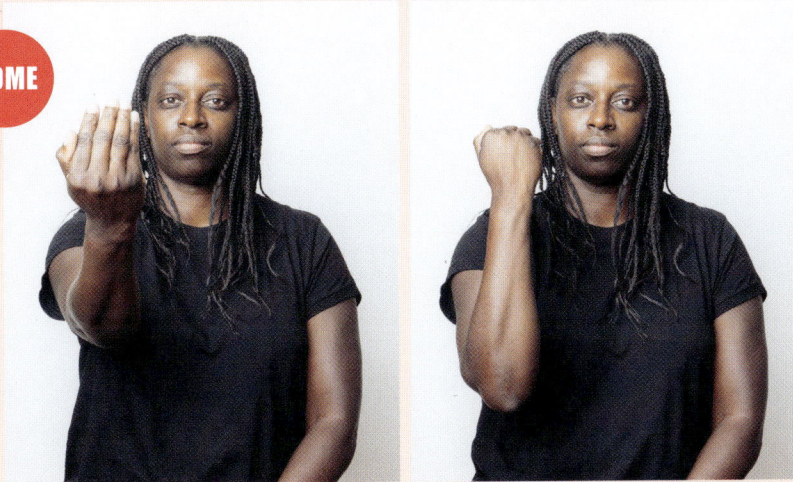

With your arm outstretched and your palm up, move your hand toward yourself in a long arch.

STAY TOO LONG

Place your hand flat, with the four fingers together and the thumb extended (flat B-handshape, page 22). With the palm toward the audience, move it quickly outward. Then point both index fingers, make them touch in the center, and move your hands in opposite arcs.

MEET

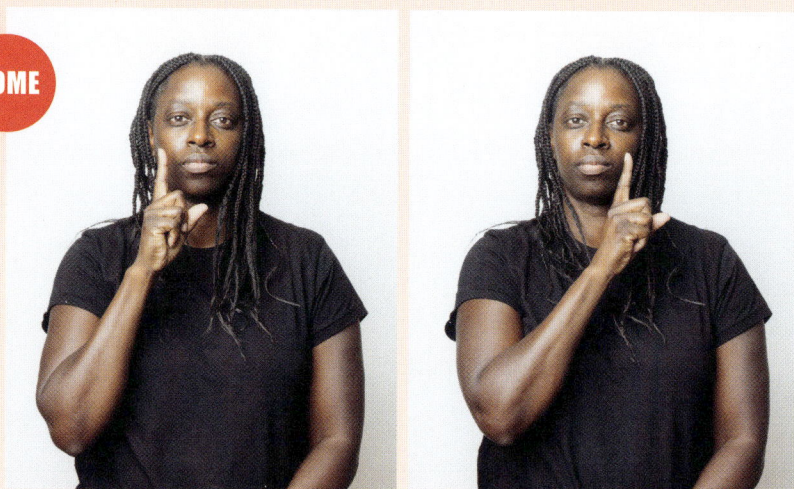

HOME

Point your index finger up and place your hand in front of your mouth. Then move your hand side to side.

RUN

HOME

Place both hands in a 5-handshape in the neutral space, with the palms facing each other. Raise the left hand slightly above the right and shake both hands toward the audience twice.

WAIT

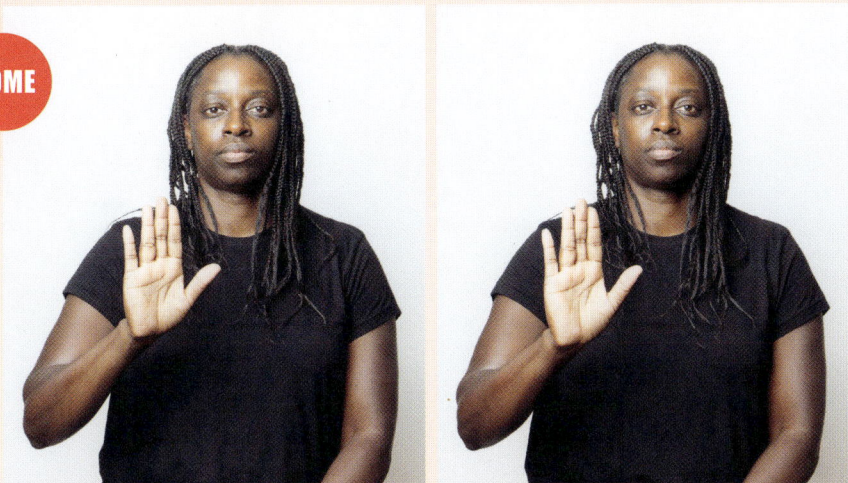

Place your hand in a 5-handshape in front of your chest, with the palm facing the audience. Then push your hand forward a few times.
Note: *The sign is similar to motioning someone to stop.*

HIDE

Place both hands in a slightly curved 5-handshape at chin level. Place the left hand horizontal with the palm facing down. Then thread the right hand under the curve of the left hand toward the audience.
Note: *The sign mimics hiding.*

PLAY

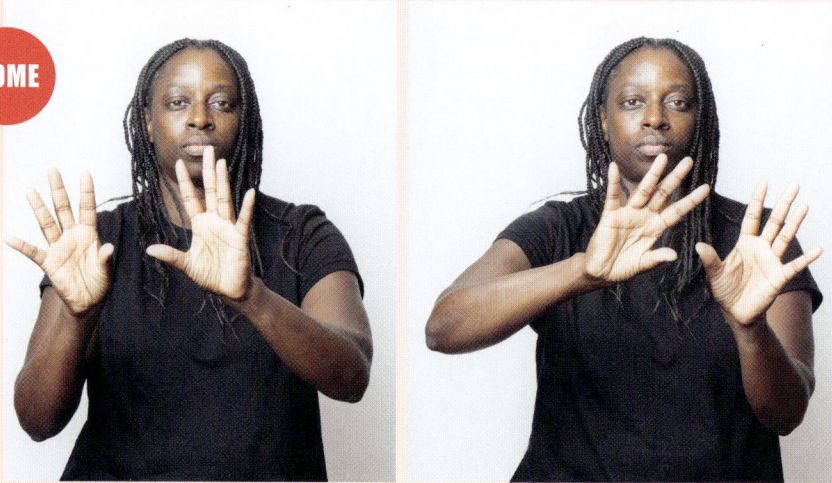

Place both hands in a spread 5-handshape in the neutral space, with the palms facing the audience, then shake them while moving the hands side to side.

DIVORCE

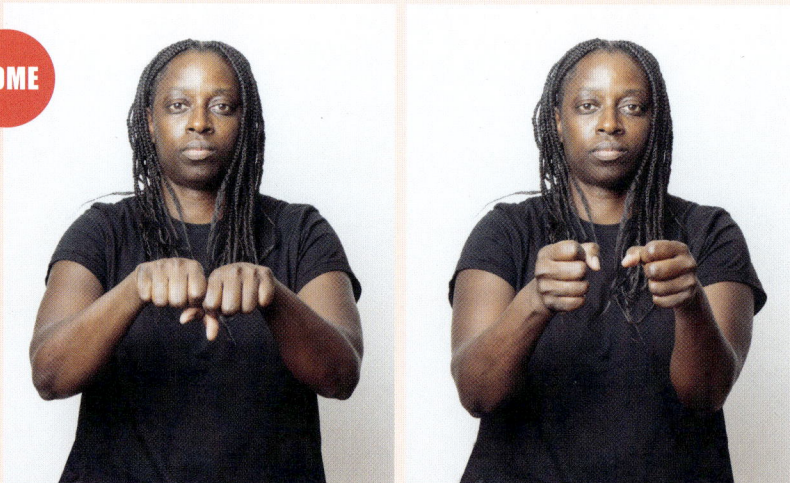

Place both hands into fists with the thumbs on top of the index fingers (S-handshapes, page 25). Touch the sides of your fists together, then rotate them 90-degrees to pull them apart. **Note:** *The sign simulates the action of something breaking.*

OPEN

HOME

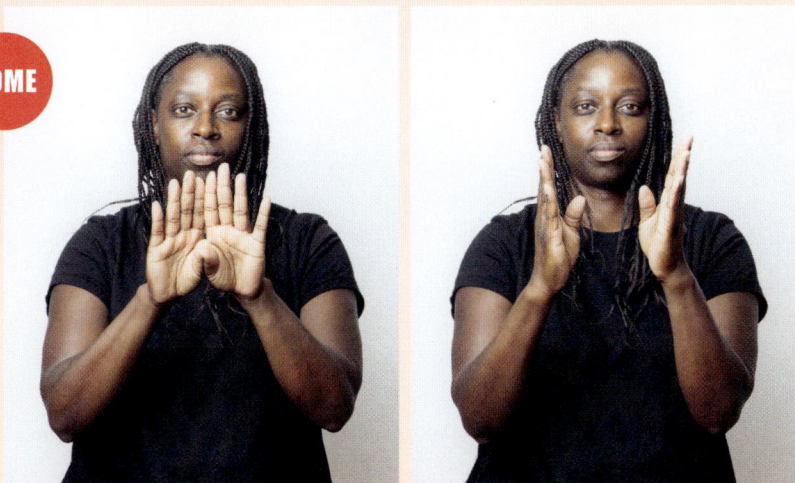

Place both hands in a 5-handshape with the palms facing the audience in the neutral space. With the index fingers slightly touching, move them in an arc that opens upward.

ASL

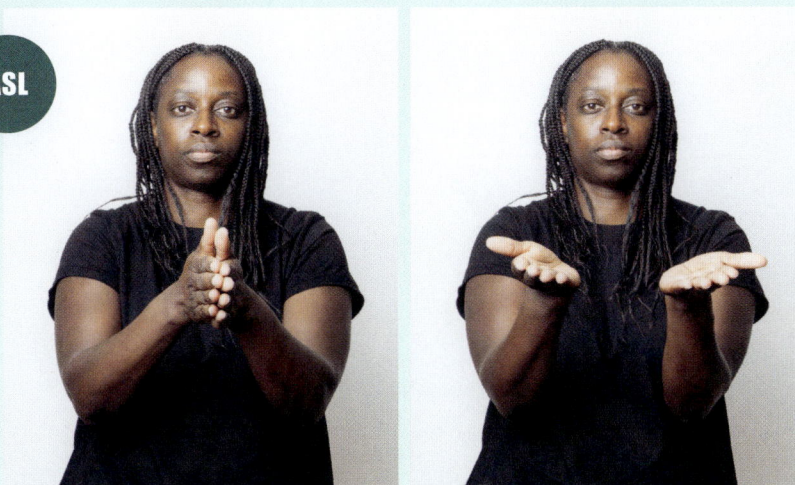

Place both hands in a 5-handshape and touch the palms together. Then spread them apart while making a small arc.

CLOSE

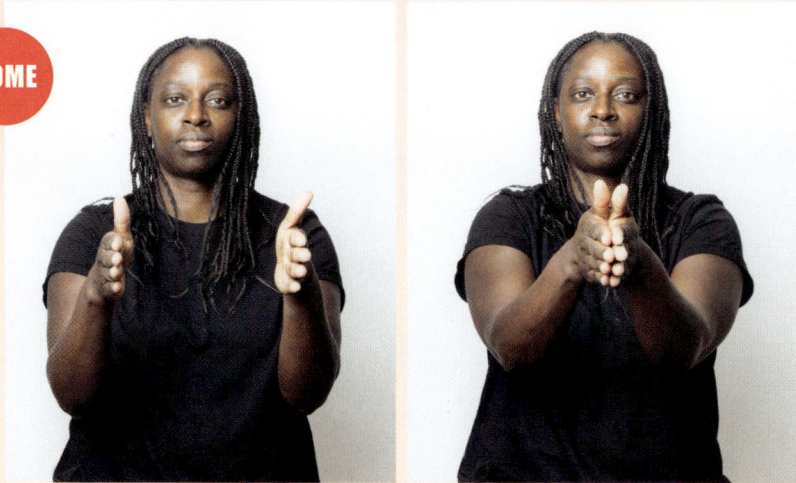

HOME

Place both hands in a 5-handshape and make contact in the neutral space.

ASL

Place both hands flat with the thumb tucked against the palm (B-handshape, page 22) in the neutral space and the palms facing up. Then simultaneously flip both hands so the palms are facing the audience and position them side by side.

LEARN BLACK AMERICAN SIGN LANGUAGE

MARRY

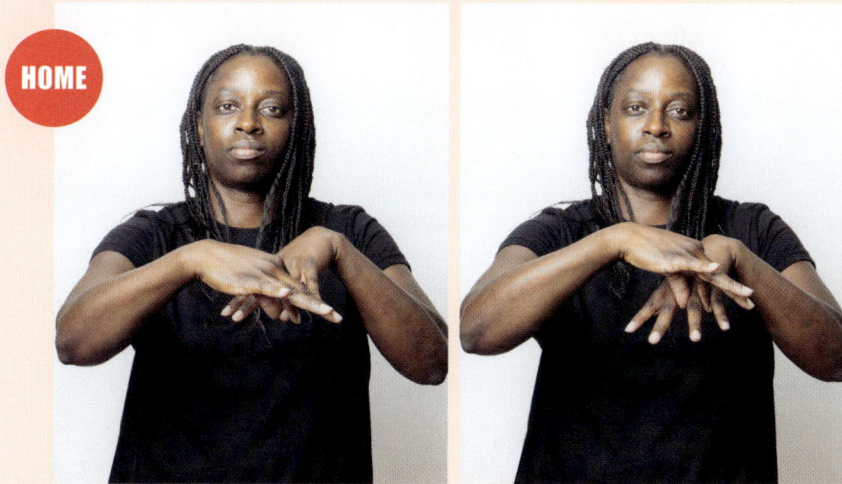

Place your left hand in a spread 5-handshape, with the palm facing down. Then use your right thumb and index finger to pinch your left ring finger.

GET ENGAGED

Place your left hand in a spread 5-handshape, with the palm facing down. Then place your right thumb and index finger on top of your left ring finger.

Franklin is signing the word *deaf* (page 164) while Stephanie is signing the word *happy* (page 156).

DESCRIPTIONS & EMOTIONS

GOOD

Make a thumbs-up with your hand and move it back and forth.

BAD

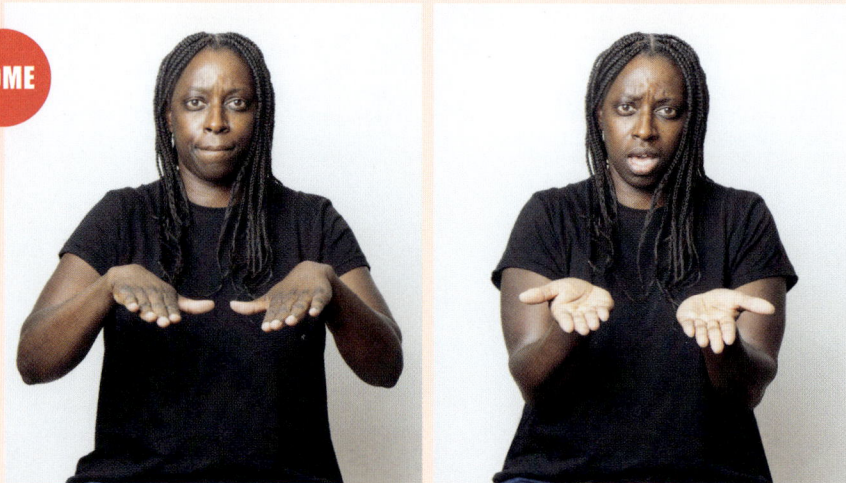

Place both hands palm down, then flip them so the palms are facing up. Make a mouth movement for "bad."

OLD

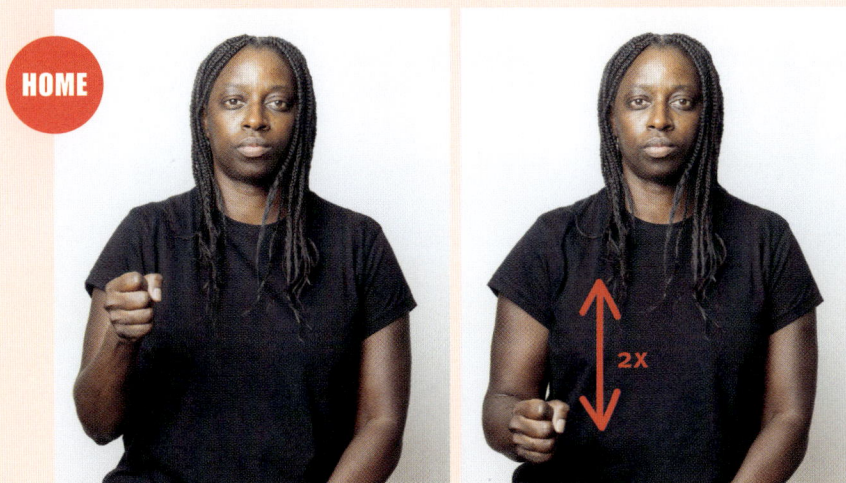

Place your hand in a fist and move it down and up twice.

NEW

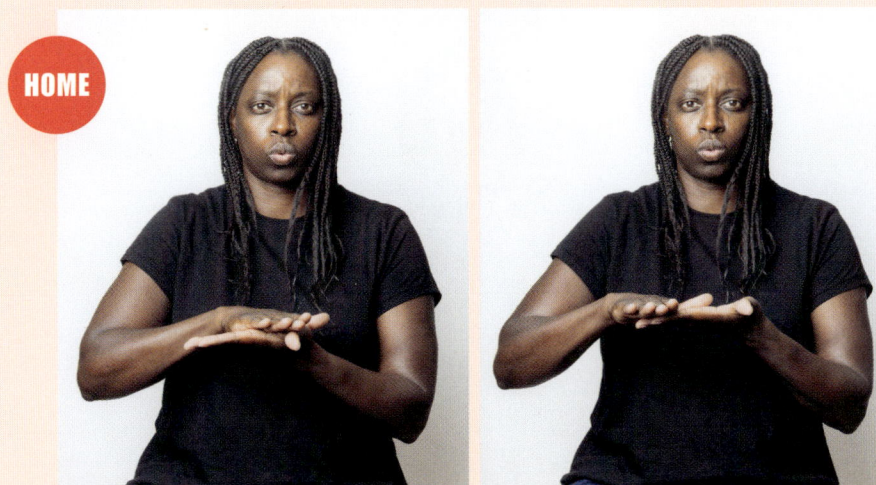

Place both hands flat with the four fingers together and the thumb extended (flat B-handshape, page 22). Touch the palms together, with the right on top of the left, and move the right hand across the palm at a diagonal.

BIG

Start with both hands close together, then pull them apart.

SMALL

Hold both hands flat with the palms facing each other and keep space between them.

SHORT

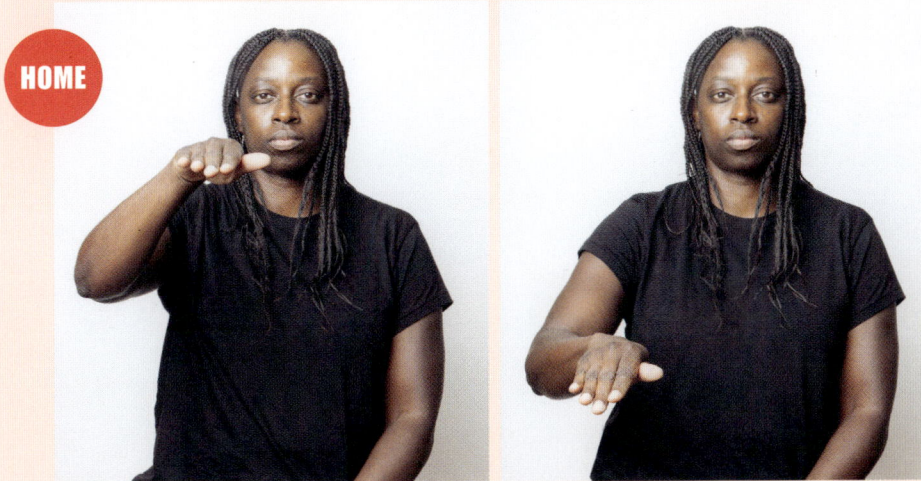

Place your hand flat in the neutral space at about eye level, with the thumb tucked under the first finger and the palm facing down. Then move your hand down in a quick, short motion.
Note: The sign describes what short looks like.

TALL

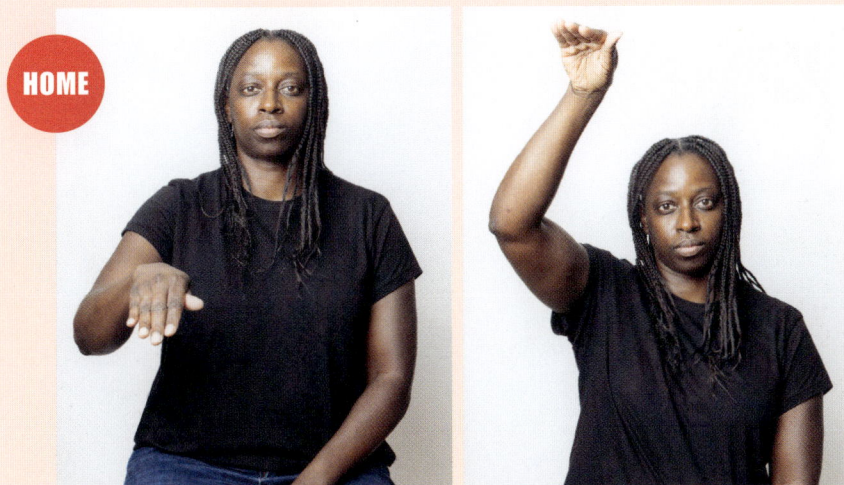

Place your hand flat in the neutral space at about chest level, with the thumb tucked under the first finger and the palm facing down. Then raise your hand until it's above your head.
Note: The sign describes what tall looks like.

SKINNY

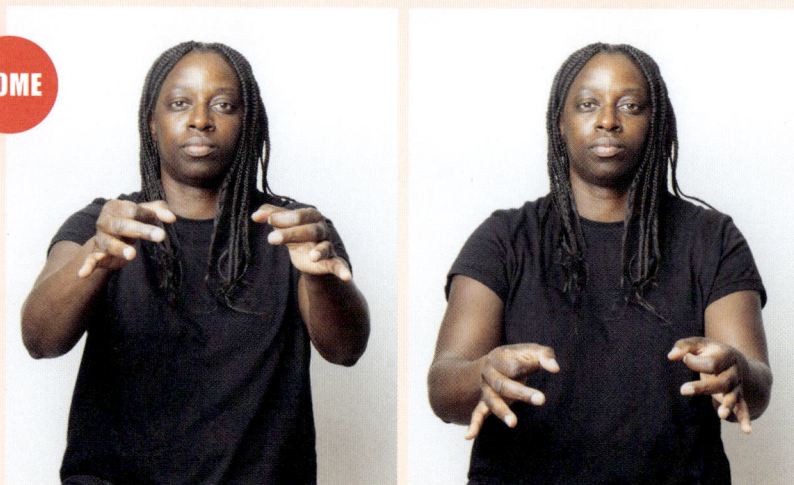

Make ovals with the index fingers and thumbs, with the rest of the fingers extended (F-handshape, page 22). Start at shoulder level in the neutral space and move your hands down.
Note: *The sign is the same for thin.*

FAT

Hold both hands in a curved 5-handshape at shoulder level, then pull your arms back while your head moves forward.

NICE

HOME

Place your hands in a 5-handshape with the palms facing down, then move your hands down and out to the sides.
Note: *The sign is the same for kind.*

MEAN

HOME

Point your index finger at the audience. Then squeeze both hands into fists and scrunch your face with a "mean" mouth movement.

BEAUTIFUL

HOME

Place your hand by the side of your face. Then sweep it over your face in a clockwise motion.
Note: The sign is the same for pretty and handsome.

HAPPY

HOME

Place both hands in a 5-handshape against the chest. Then sweep the hands upward toward the chin twice.

UGLY VIRGINIA

Place your index finger at nose level, with your thumb extended and the rest of the fingers closed. Then curl your index finger while slightly rotating your hand.

Place your index finger under the side of the nose, then move it horizontally. While your hand is moving, bend your finger into a hook (X-handshape, page 26).

SAD

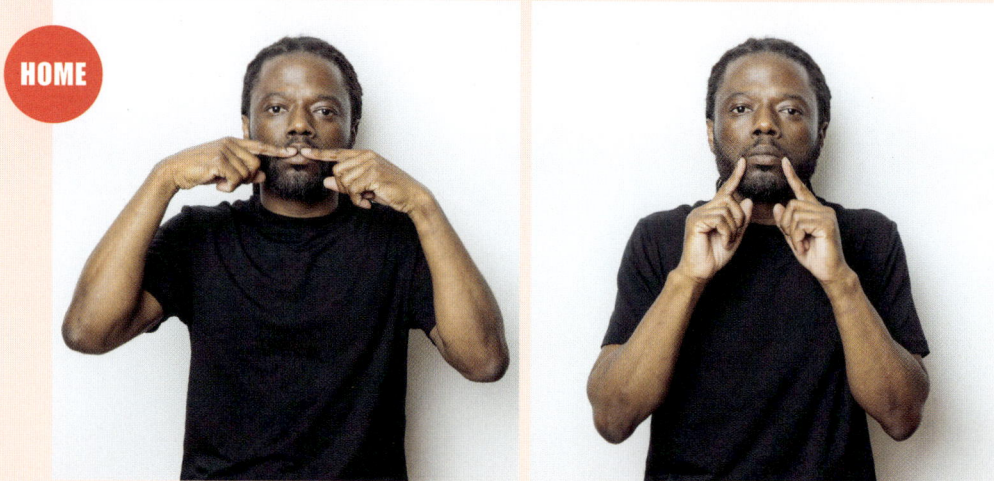

Touch both index fingers to the crease between your lips, then trace them down in an arc toward your chin.

HATE

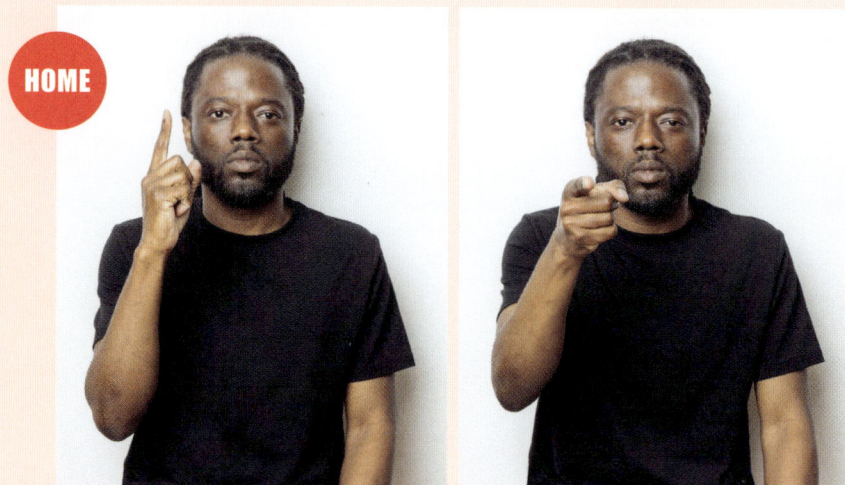

Point your index finger in the air and swing it toward the audience.

LOVE (PLATONIC)

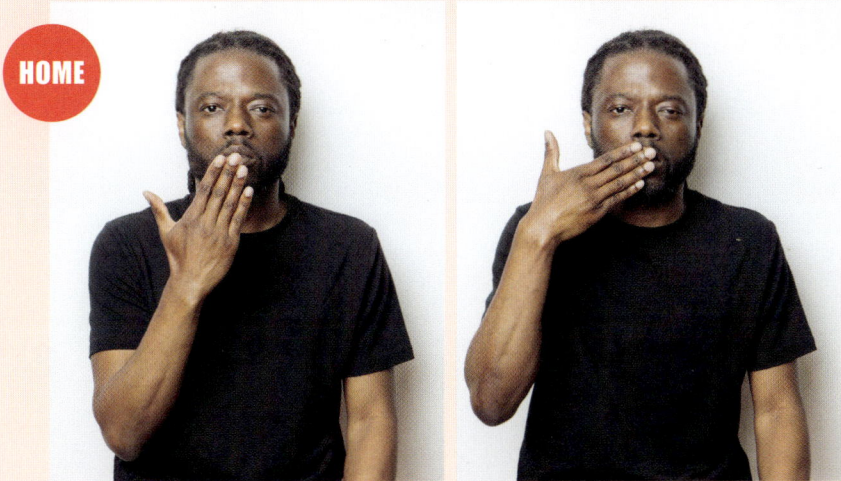

HOME

Place your hand flat, with the four fingers together and the thumb extended (flat B-handshape, page 22) and the palm facing you. Move your hand toward you and touch your lips.
Note: The sign also indicates a familial love.

ASL

Place both hands in a fist and form an X with your arms in the neutral space. Then move them toward your body and touch your upper chest.

GRUMPY

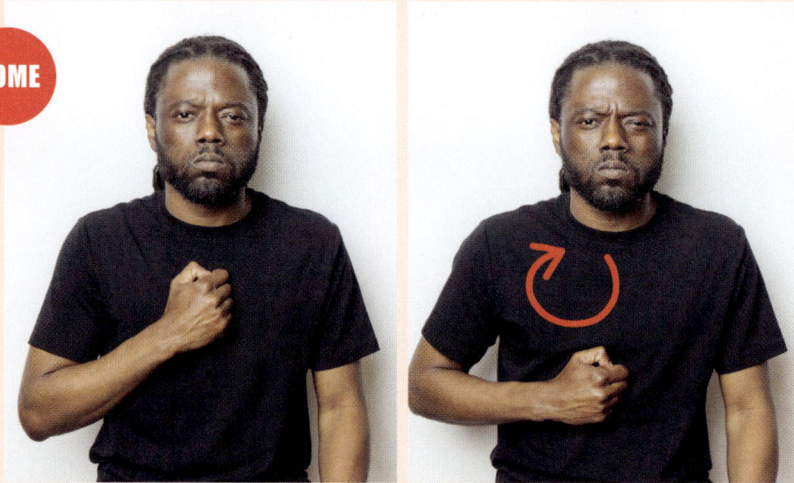

Form a fist with your hand and move in a small circular motion on your chest. **Note:** *Make a grumpy facial expression.*

ANGRY

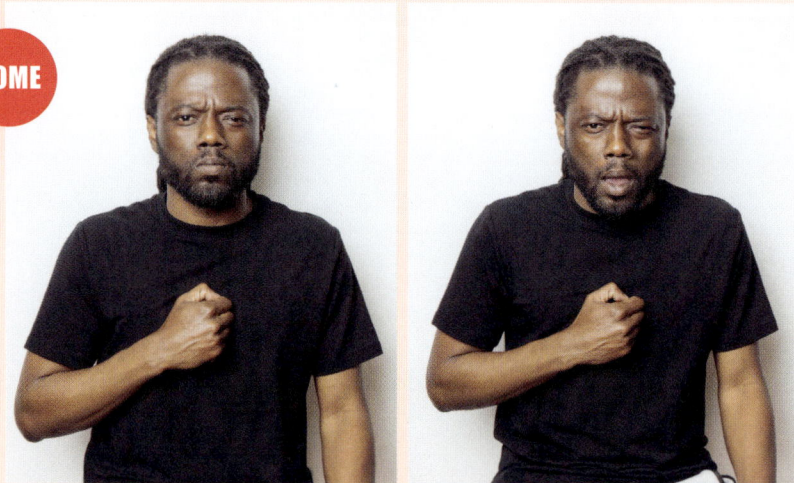

Form a fist with your hand and rest it against your chest as you push your head forward and make a "mad" mouth movement.

HURT

Cradle your right hand, with the palm facing up, in your left hand.
Note: The sign indicates physical pain. Use facial expressions to convey the meaning of the word.

HARD

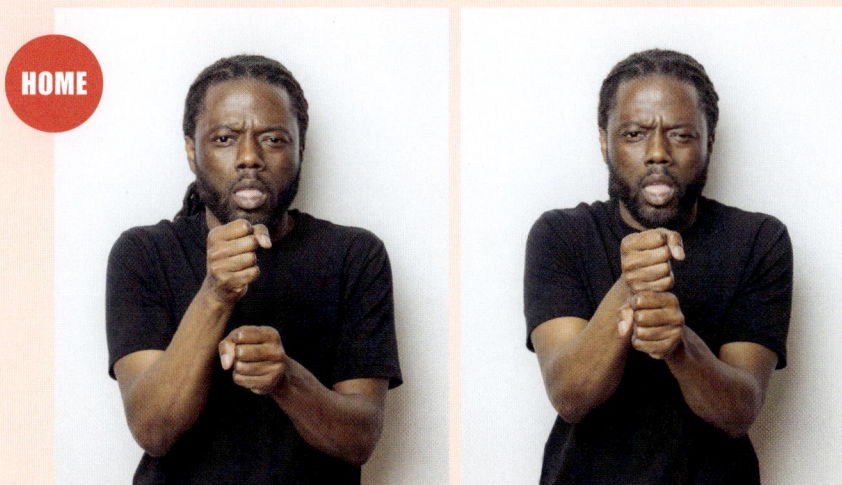

Place your left hand in a fist and keep it still. With your right hand also in a fist, move it up and down while tapping the side of the left fist.
Note: Make a facial expression showing difficulty.

SLOW

Place both hands in a 5-handshape with the fingers spread. Then move your hands down slowly in the neutral space with a "slow" mouth movement.

FAST

Place both hands flat with the four fingers together and the thumb extended (flat B-handshape, page 22). Hold them in the neutral space with the palms facing each other. Then touch the right hand to the left hand and move it toward the audience.

HUNGRY

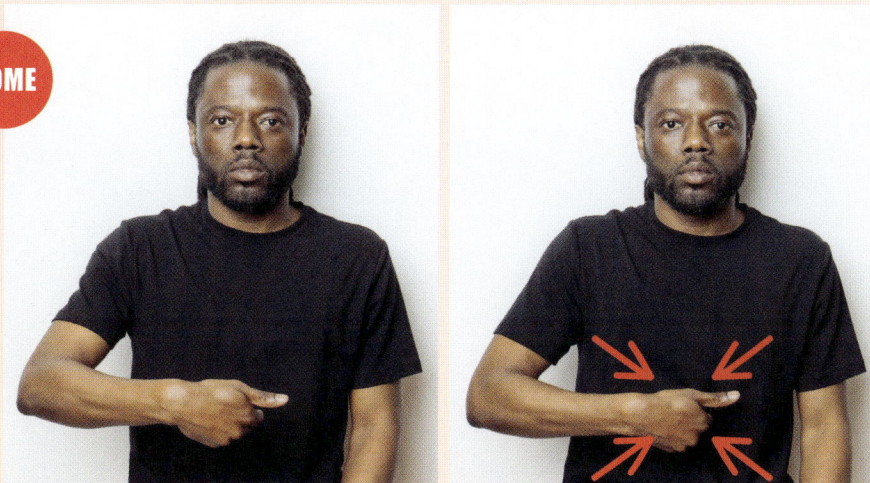

HOME

Place your hand flat with the four fingers together and the thumb extended (B-handshape, page 22) and curve it toward you at stomach level. Then push your fingers against the stomach.

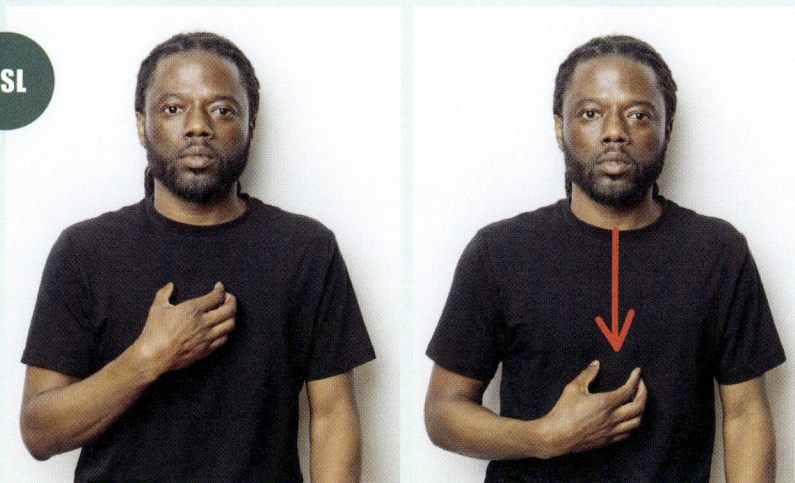

ASL

Place your hand in a C shape (C-handshape, page 22) and touch your upper chest, then move your hand down toward the stomach area.

DEAF

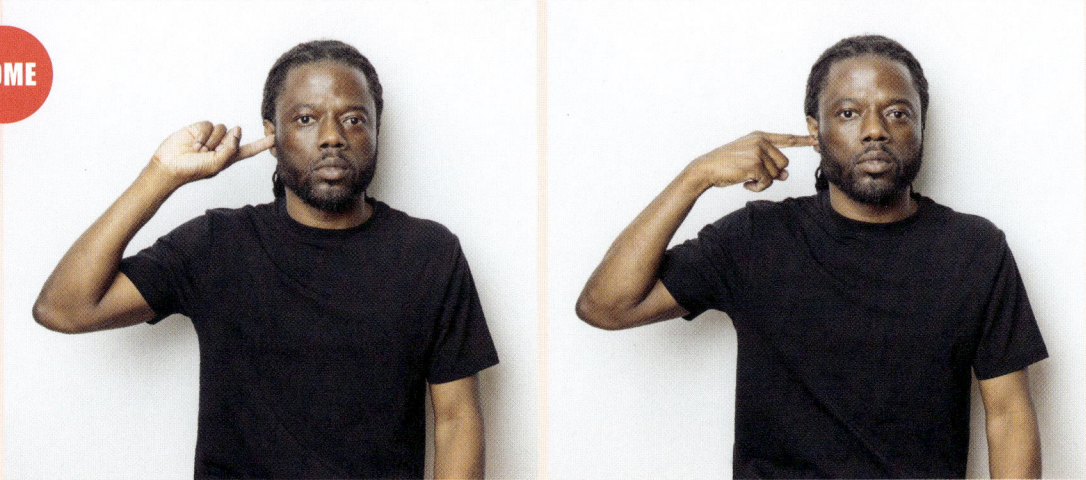

Place your index finger in your ear. Then twist your finger forward until your palm faces away from the audience.

WHITE

Place the hand flat with the four fingers together and the thumb extended (flat B-handshape, page 22). With the palm facing the side of the head, move it back toward the ear twice.
Note: *The sign refers to a "white person."*

BLACK

HOME

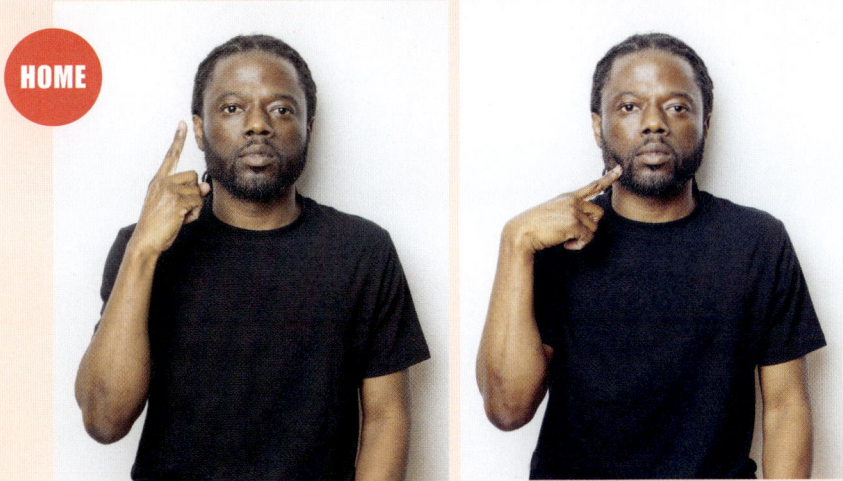

Place your index finger against your cheek, then move it downward.
Note: *The sign refers to a Black person.*

LIGHT-SKINNED

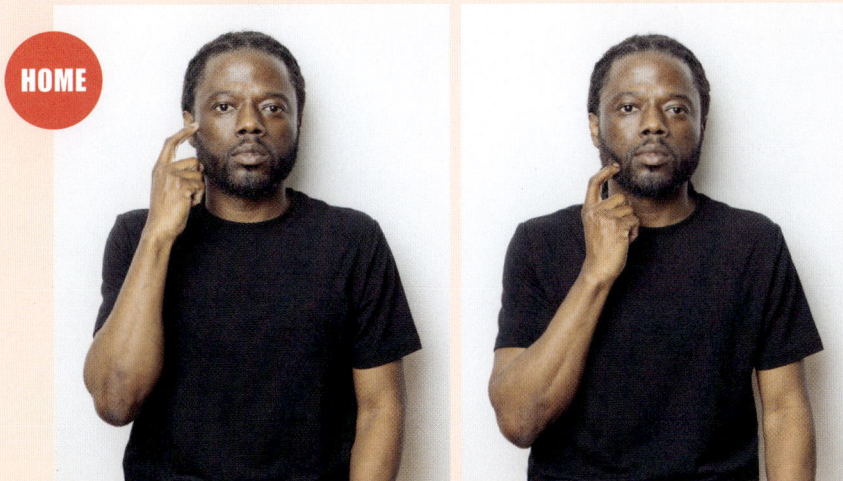

HOME

Slightly bend your index finger and touch the side of your face. Then drag your finger down to your chin.

Franklin is signing the phrase *I'm down* (page 170) while Stephanie is signing the word *yass* (page 176).

AFRICAN AMERICAN VERNACULAR ENGLISH (AAVE)

#HEY

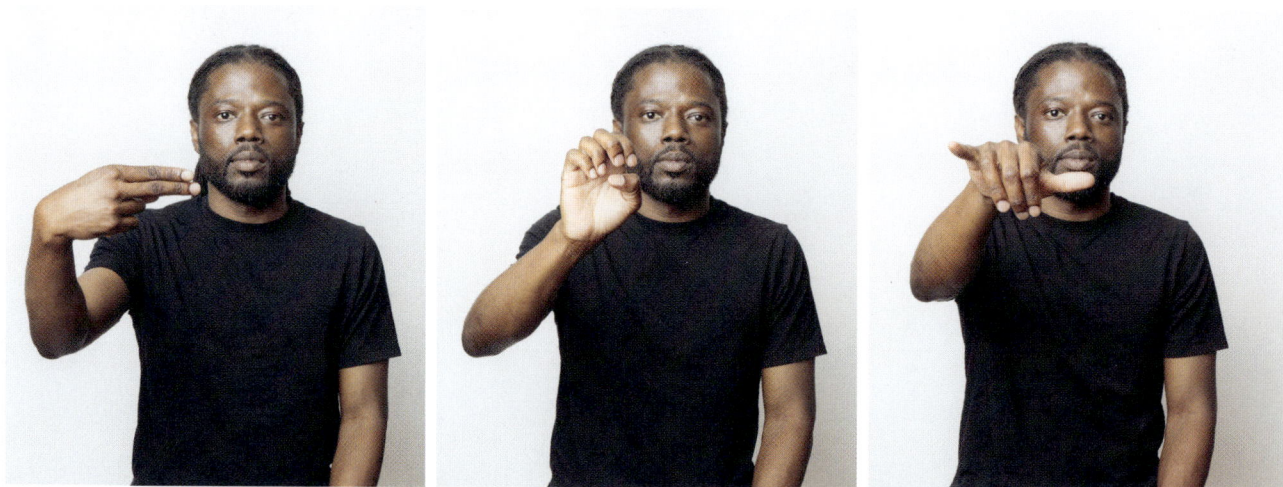

Spell "hey" with a downward swing and mouth movement. First, extend your first two fingers with the rest of the fingers curled (H-handshape, page 23). Then curve all your fingers, keeping a space between your fingertips and thumb (E-handshape, page 22). Finally, curl your three middle fingers and extend the thumb and pinky (Y-handshape, page 26) while making a "hey" mouth movement.

#YO

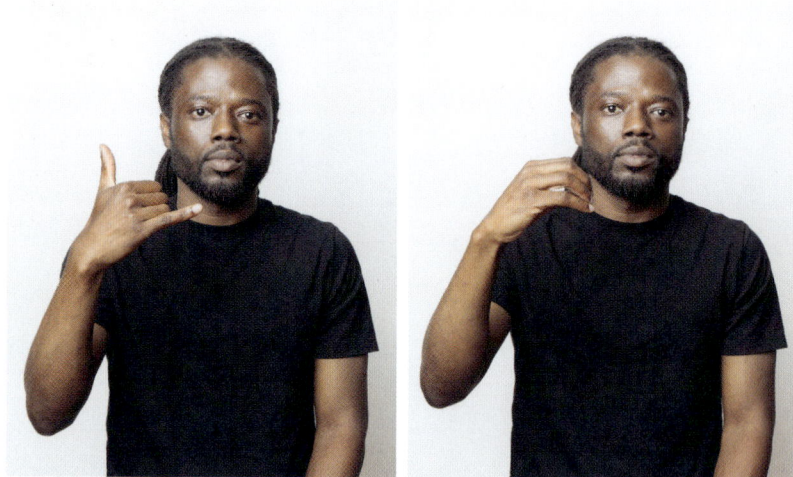

Spell "yo" with a swing. Extend your thumb and pinky with the rest of the fingers curled (Y-handshape, page 26). Then position your hand so your palm is facing you. Finally, swing your hand down and touch all your fingers together to make a circle (O-handshape, page 24).

WHAT'S UP?

Touch your chest with both middle fingers, then move both hands up with an upward head nod.

I FEEL YOU

Touch your middle fingers to the middle of your chest and sweep your hand up. Then point your index finger at the audience.

I'M DOWN

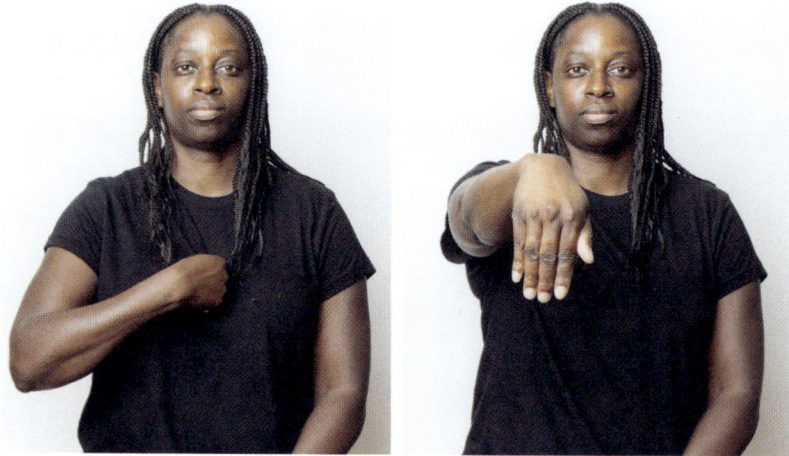

Point to yourself in the middle of your chest. Then with a 5-handshape, the thumb extended, and the hand slightly bent, gesture in a downward angle in the neutral space.

I GOT YOU

Point your index finger at yourself, then make both hands a fist. Tap the sides of your fists together once and point your index finger at the audience.

GIRL, PLEASE

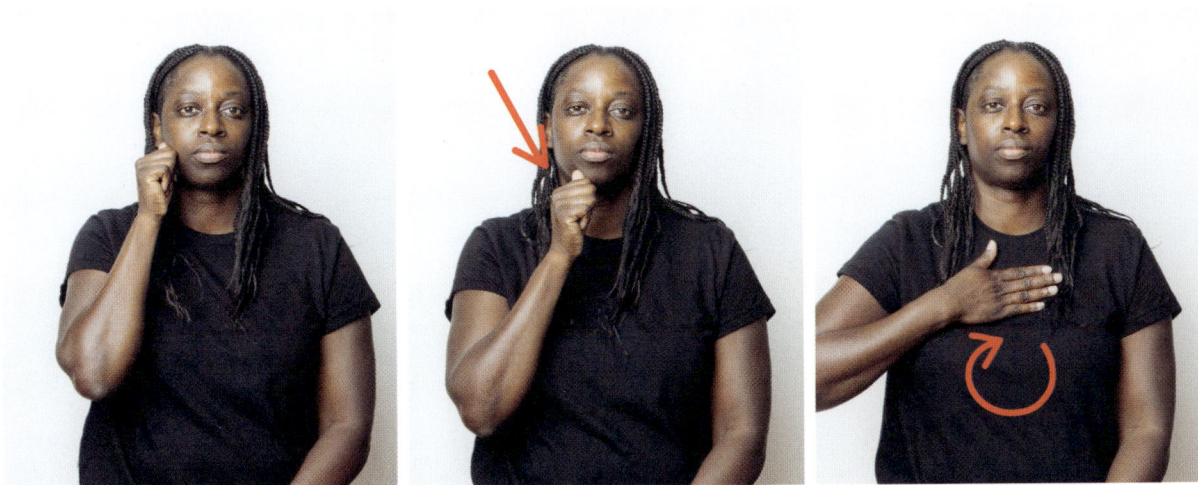

Place your fist with your thumb sticking out at the side of your head and drag your thumb along your jaw. Then make a 5-handshape with your hand and make a clockwise motion over your chest.

STOP PLAYIN'

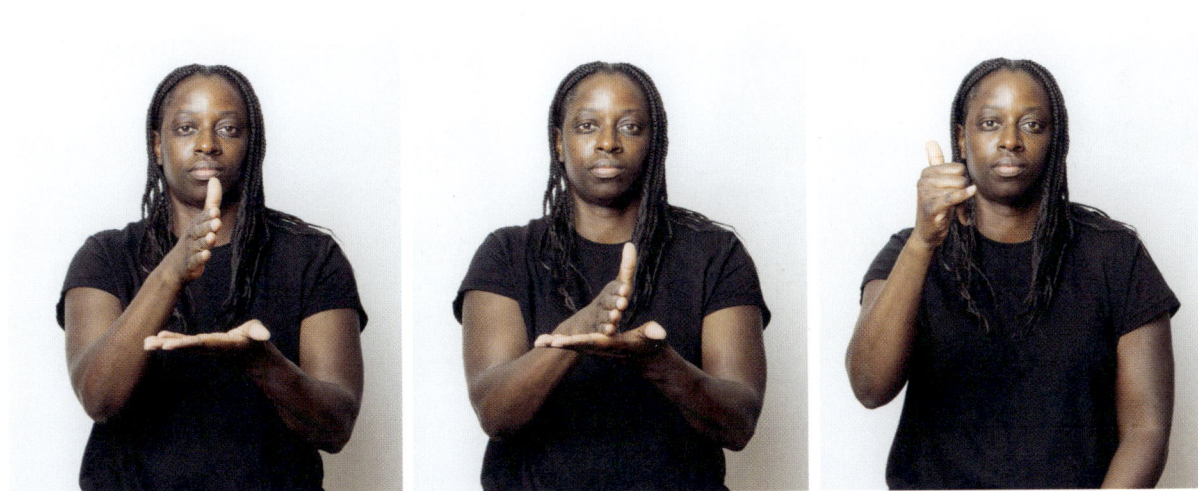

Place your left hand palm up in front of you. Then with your right hand flat, tap the side of it to the palm of your left hand. Finally, in the neutral space, curl the three middle fingers of your right hand with your pinky and thumb extended (Y-handshape, page 26).

I AIN'T PLAYIN'

Brush your thumb under your chin. Then extend the pinky and thumb (Y-handshape, page 26) and shake them in the neutral space with a headshake.

YOU FINE

Point your index finger at the audience. Then, with both hands in a fist and the thumbs extended and facing each other, rotate your hands up and then back down.

STOP TRIPPIN' VERSION 1

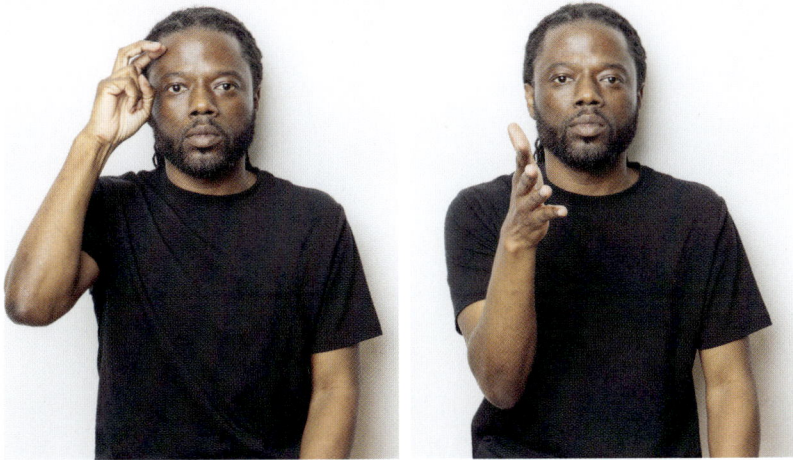

Bend your index and middle fingers and touch them to the side of your head twice. Then move your hand to the neutral space, spread your fingers in a 5-handshape, and twist your hand, left to right, in a small movement.

STOP TRIPPIN' VERSION 2

Hold your left hand flat with the palm facing up. Place your right hand flat, with the four fingers together and the thumb extended (flat B-handshape, page 22) and tap the side of the hand against the left palm. Then keep your first two fingers and thumb extended and slightly curved while tapping the side of the forehead twice.

#FOOL

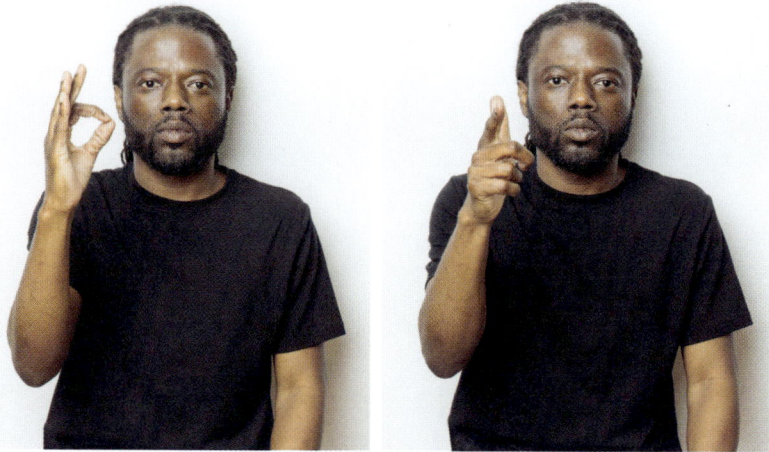

Spell "F-L" by first making an oval with your index finger and thumb with the rest of the fingers extended (F-handshape, page 22). Then quickly extend your index finger and thumb and curl the other fingers to make a 90-degree angle.

#HOOD

Spell "hood" while sliding your hand to the left. First, extend the first two fingers with the rest of the fingers curled (H-handshape, page 24). Then make a circle with your hand so your fingertips touch (O-handshape, page 24) and slide it to the side. Then quickly extend the index finger while keeping the rest of your fingertips together (D-handshape, page 22). Meanwhile make a mouth movement of "hood."

#BAD

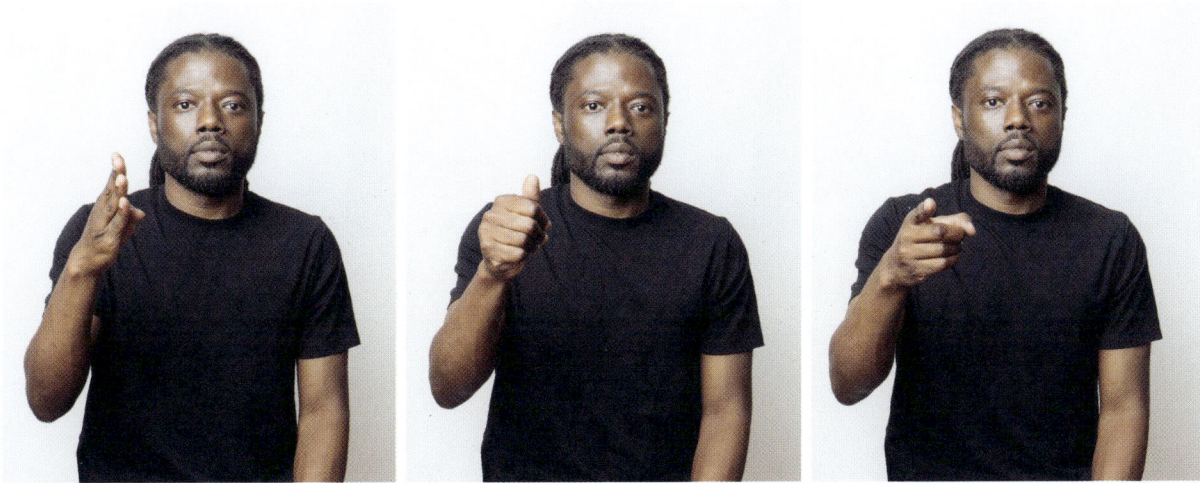

Spell "bad" by making your hand flat with the four fingers together and the thumb folded (B-handshape, page 22). Then make a fist (A-handshape, page 22). Then keep all your fingers in a fist but extend the index finger (D-handshape, page 22). Meanwhile stick your tongue out and make the mouth movement for "bad."

#BRUH

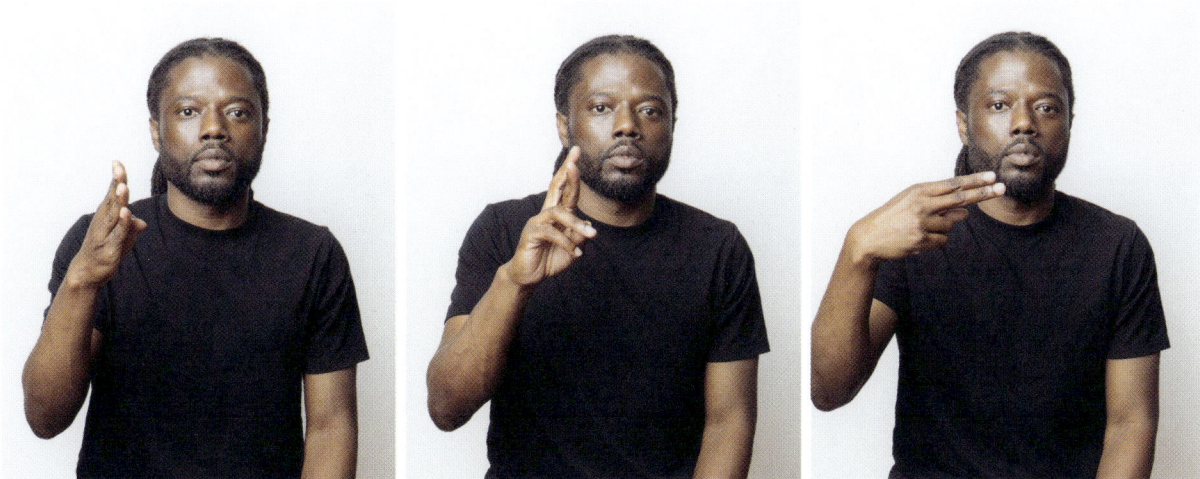

Spell "bruh" by placing your hand flat, with the four fingers together and the thumb folded (B-handshape, page 22) and pointing at the audience. Then cross your first two fingers (R-handshape, page 23). Then straighten your fingers side by side (U-handshape, page 25) and turn your hand horizontal (H-handshape, page 24) while making a mouth movement for "brother." This finger spelling can be signed so fast that you can't see the letter U.

TIGHT

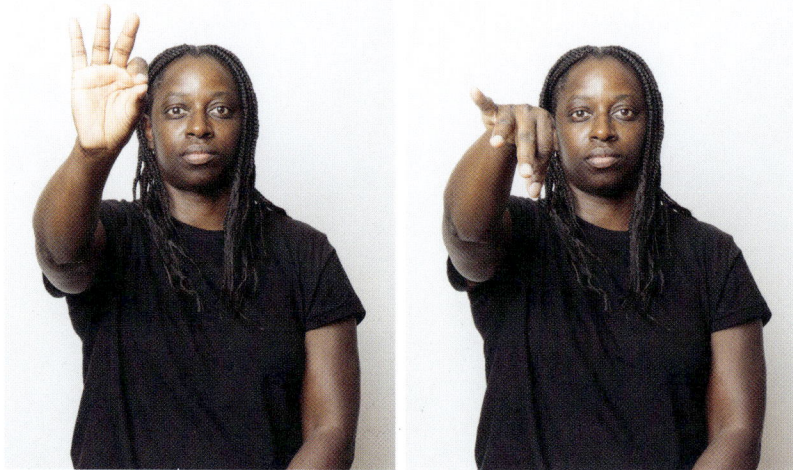

Place your index finger and thumb together while the other fingers are extended (F-handshape, page 22). Then quickly flick your wrist to move your fingers down and up.

#YASS

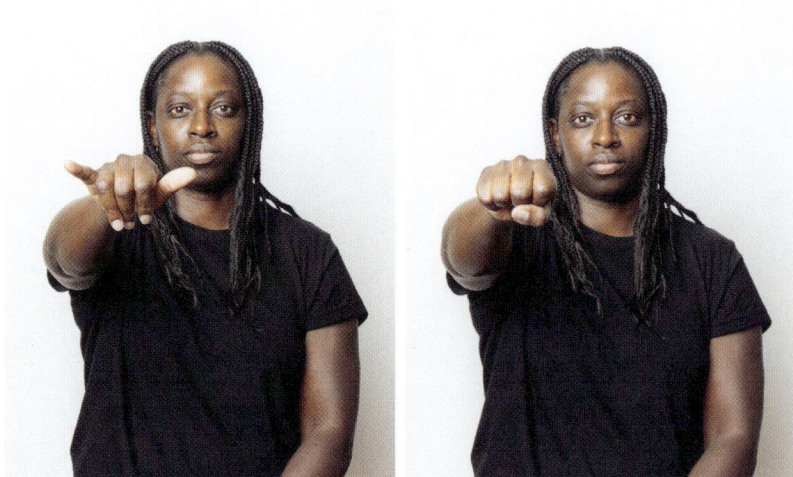

Spell "Y-S." Curl the three middle fingers of both hands with the pinky and thumb extended (Y-handshape, page 26). Then close your hands in a fist (S-handshape, page 25) while making a mouth movement of "yass."

DOPE

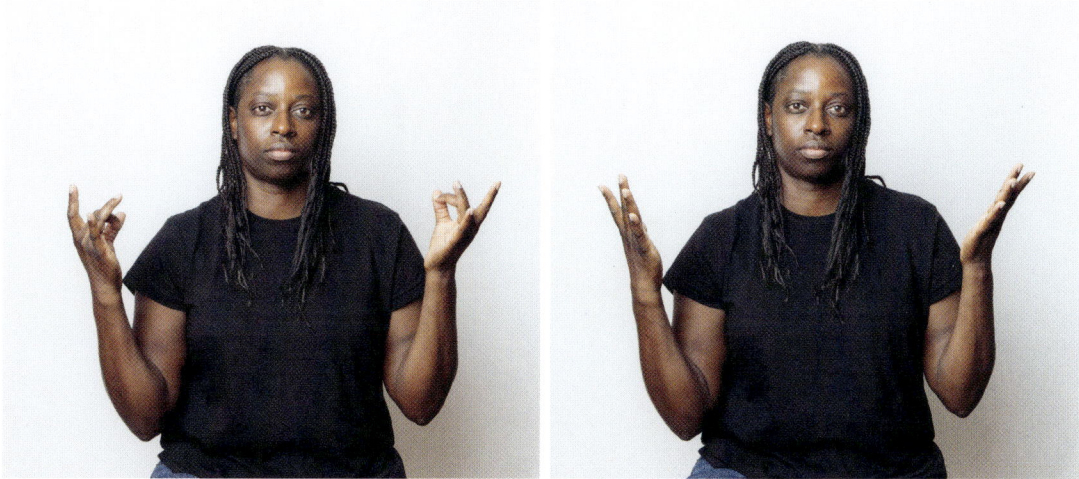

Touch both middle fingers and thumbs together, with the rest of the fingers extended. Then flick your middle fingers twice in the neutral space.

LOWKEY

Place both hands in a 5-handshape and move them up and down twice.

HELLA

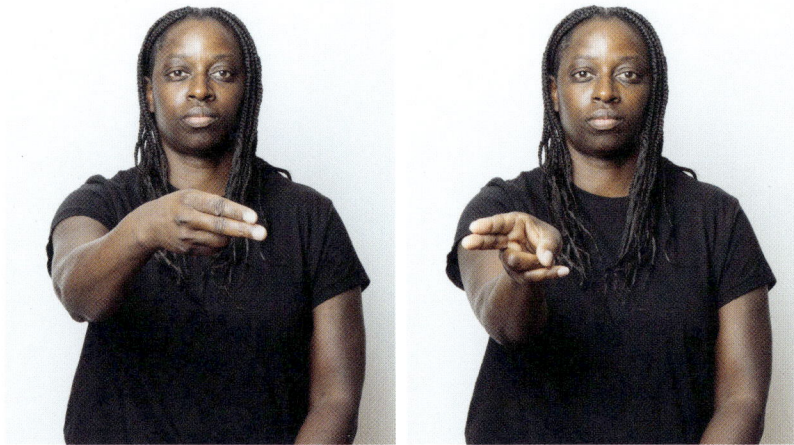

Extend your first two fingers and curl the rest of your fingers (H-handshape, page 23). Move it from left to right and flip your hand so the palm is facing the audience. Meanwhile make the mouth movement "hella."

REAL TALK

Touch your index finger to your chin, with your fingers curled. Then move your hand to the neutral space at forehead level and curve it into a C shape (C-handshape, page 22). Open and close your fingers in a quick, repetitive motion.

CRAY CRAY

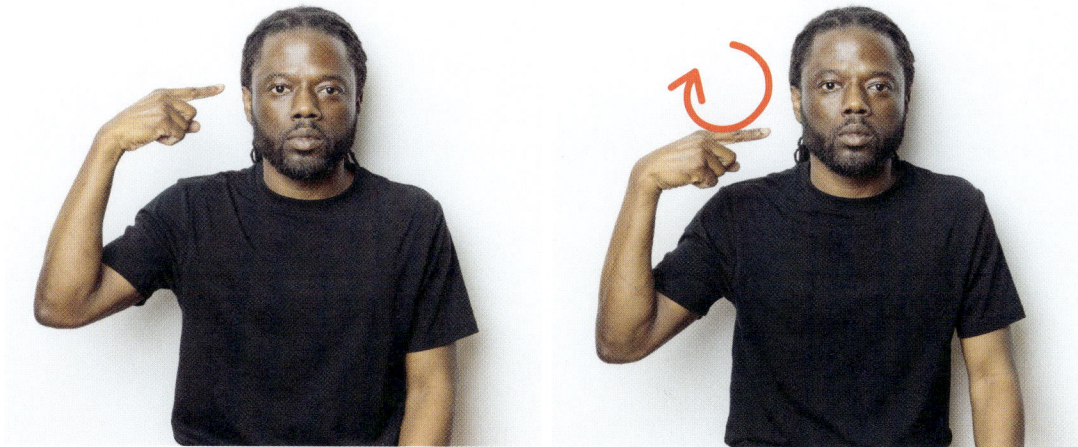

Point your index finger to your ear, then move it in a circular motion.

FO' SHO'

Point your index finger to the side of your head and move it forward to the neutral space.
Then touch your chin and move it toward the audience.

WERK

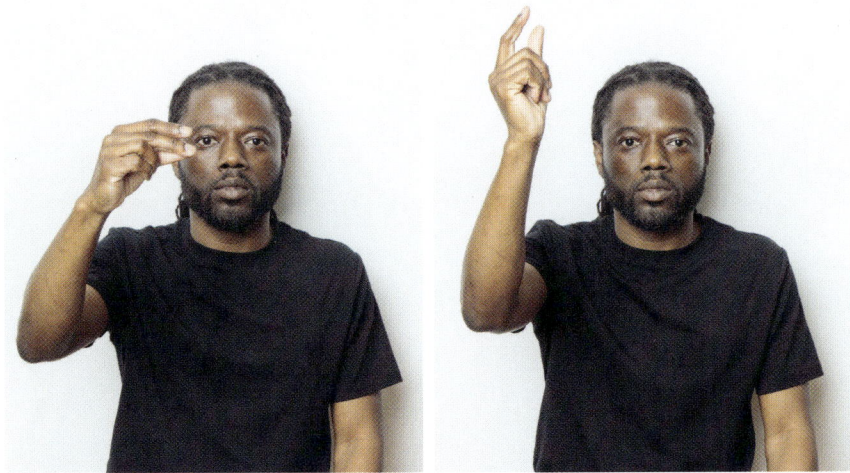

Place your thumb and middle finger together, then snap twice: to the left and to the right.

SLAY

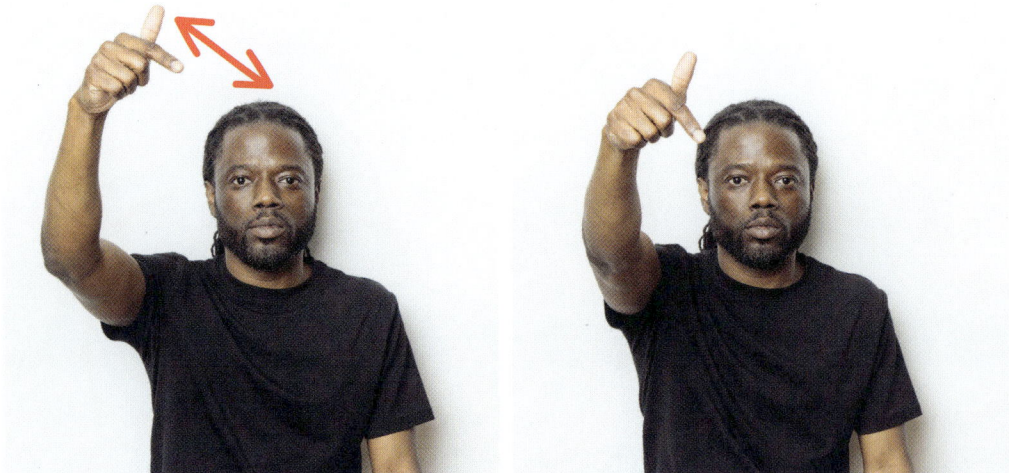

With your hand above your head, point your finger downward and gesture toward the neutral space repeatedly.

LEARN BLACK AMERICAN SIGN LANGUAGE

Black American Sign Language Today

Is Black American Sign Language (BASL) dying? No. BASL still exists; however, its use is gradually dwindling within the Black Deaf community. Many of us continue to embrace it through discussion, both nationally and internationally, and to show our cultural pride, but newer generations are increasingly shifting toward ASL, with some influenced by African American Vernacular English (AAVE).

On the other hand, many young Black Deaf people—especially those who have never experienced segregation—are not exposed to BASL today. This is partly because there are not many Black teachers or role models consistently using BASL in front of them. Additionally, many elders have either passed away or forgotten their BASL because they stopped using it years ago. Instead, new generations are more often exposed to standardized ASL or AAVE-based signing.

Today, BASL's linguistic features have changed, and it does not look the same as it did before desegregation. Following desegregation, BASL was often blended with standardized ASL as Deaf schools and spaces like dormitories and social events integrated. Still, some Black Deaf individuals from multigenerational Deaf families continue to use BASL daily. Even now, you will find those in the Black Deaf community who maintain it as part of their identity and communication style.

Desegregation increased contact among racially and culturally diverse Deaf communities, which allowed standard ASL and AAVE to exert greater influence. Since Deaf individuals from Deaf families are relatively rare, BASL has been preserved by a small group. Today, most Black Deaf signers are influenced by their cultures, linguistic environments, personal experiences, and community norms, while a committed few continue to uphold traditional BASL. One such voice is Nakia Smith, a.k.a. Charmay, a Deaf advocate and fourth Deaf generation of five. She went viral on TikTok (@itscharmay) when she posted a video about the differences between BASL and ASL. She has since been featured as a Strong Black Lead for the YouTube channel Still Watching Netflix and continues to share BASL content on her social media platforms.

CJ Jones at the Hollywood premiere of *See What I'm Saying*, March 2010.

Another voice is CEO, actor, and comedian CJ Jones has used his career in the entertainment industry for the betterment of the Deaf community. He made his feature film debut in Edgar Wright's 2017 blockbuster *Baby Driver* playing Joseph, Ansel Elgort's Deaf foster father. He also created the Na'vi Sign Language (NSL) for James Cameron's movie *Avatar 2*.

Understanding a person's background, such as where they grew up, whether they were raised in Deaf or hearing families, and their language exposure, is key to understanding their communication style. AAVE is now widely used in the Black Deaf community, particularly among those born into hearing families. These individuals often absorb their families' expressions and social cues, which influence how they sign. There are also cases when ASL interpreters are needed for social events and entertainment, and so, ASL can also be adapted for performances. Take, for example, American Sign Language performers Justina Miles and Matt Maxey, who have become Black ASL public figures in the music space.

Justina Miles performs "Lift Every Voice and Sing" in American Sign Language prior to Super Bowl LVII at State Farm Stadium in Glendale, Arizona.

In 2023, Deaflympics athlete and American Sign Language performer Justina Miles became the first Black Deaf woman to perform ASL at the Super Bowl pregame show. She was also the ASL performer for Rihanna's halftime show and wowed viewers with her passion and energy. Matt Maxey is the founder of Deafinitely Dope, an ASL interpreter and performance group for live music events. He is Chance the Rapper's personal interpreter for his live shows, which then got him noticed by rapper Kendrick Lamar. After seeing him in action, Lamar personally requested that Maxey be his ASL performer for his 2025 Super Bowl Halftime show, showcasing Maxey's specialty for interpreting fast and difficult song lyrics.

Many Black Deaf people also code-switch when interacting with Deaf individuals to ensure mutual understanding, though this does not apply to everyone. It is important not to assume that all Black Deaf people use BASL; we are not a monolith. Some use BASL, some use AAVE-influenced ASL, and others blend or shift between the two depending on context. In some instances, Deaf individuals may choose to speak instead of sign. Former Deaf professional baseball player Curtis Pride often speaks in interviews. In an interview for the MLB Network covering his autobiography *I Felt the Cheers: The Remarkable Silent Life of Curtis Pride*, he claimed that he rarely signed with his teammates during his time in the major leagues, and instead got by vocally or using common gestures on the field.

Some question whether BASL used by Black Deaf people never part of a segregated school system can still be considered BASL. Should we call it BASL even though the signs now look different? And what do we call AAVE—a language categorized as English—when it's signed?

The Hidden Treasure of Black ASL: Its History and Structure explains how BASL developed during segregation and how it differs from other signing systems based on linguistic features and social history. It's important to remember that BASL and AAVE are distinct. BASL was created during segregation when Black Deaf students developed a rich, expressive signing system with unique features. AAVE, on the other hand, evolved within the Black hearing community and now influences how many Black Deaf individuals sign today.

No matter the form, BASL or AAVE-influenced ASL, it all still lives within the Black Deaf community. We carry multiple language influences from our history, our families, and our evolving cultural identity. Like all languages, sign language evolves. Modern technology has given people access to new vocabulary, styles, and ways to connect. Social media, community interaction, and geographic and cultural factors all contribute to this ongoing evolution. While some older BASL signs remain, many have been adapted or replaced to reflect contemporary life in the United States.

Black American Sign Language may continue to dwindle, but we will never forget its history. AAVE will carry the Black Deaf community forward, helping our language thrive because it is ours. It is a reflection of our unique identity.

Curtis Pride of the Los Angeles Angels of Anaheim on the field on August 17, 2006.

References

Berke, Jamie. "The Milan Conference of 1880: When Sign Language Was Almost Destroyed," *Verywell Health*, June 16, 2023. https://www.verywellhealth.com/deaf-history-milan-1880-1046547#:~:text=In%20 1880%2C%20there%20was%20a,for%20 the%20Deaf%20was%20banned.

Crosby, Emilye. "Civil Rights Act and Voting Rights Act." https://www.civilrightsteaching.org/resource/ civil-rights-act-and-voting-rights-act.

Gallaudet University. "Oral Education as Emancipation." https://gallaudet.edu/museum/exhibits/ history-through-deaf-eyes/language-and-identity/oral-education-as-emancipation/.

HISTORY.com Editors. "Jim Crow Laws: Definition, Facts & Timeline." HISTORY, February 28, 2018. https://www.history.com/topics/early-20th-century-us/jim-crow-laws.

Law, Spencer. "Deaf History and Culture in the United States." *VPM*, March 30, 2021. https://www.vpm.org/2021-03-30/deaf-history-and-culture-in-the-united-states.

McCaskill, C., Ceil Lucas, Robert Bayley, Joseph Christopher Hill, Roxanne Dummett, Pamela Baldwin, and Randall Hogue. *The Hidden Treasure of Black ASL: Its History and Structure* Gallaudet University Press, 2020.

PBS. "The Civil War and Emancipation." https://www.pbs.org/wgbh/aia/part4/ 4p2967.html.

Smith, A., Walt Wolfram, and Danica Cullinan. "Chapter 5: Code Switching." In *Viewers' Discussion Guide to Signing Black in America*. TALKING BLACK in AMERICA, 2025. https://www.talkingblackinamerica. org/wp-content/uploads/2020/06/ SBiA27ViewersGuide_CH5.pdf.

Index

Acknowledgments

I am deeply honored and humbled to have written this book. This journey would not have been possible without many people's support, guidance, and encouragement.

First and foremost, I want to thank my editors, Elizabeth and Katey; Cara; and the whole team at Quarto. Thank you for giving me the opportunity and believing in this project, for your patience with my busy schedule, and for pushing me to make this book happen. Your dedication helped make this celebration of Black American Sign Language in the Black Deaf community possible.

Thank you to Dr. Carolyn McCaskill for her invaluable contribution. Her part in this book, sharing her experience of segregation, brings an essential and powerful perspective. I truly appreciate her wisdom.

I also want to express my sincere appreciation to my family—my mom, Louise; my aunts, Donna, Sharon, and Blondell; my second cousin, Allen; and my third cousin, David—for your help in ensuring the accuracy of our Home signs were authentic. To my good friend Vyron, thank you for your guidance and feedback on African American Vernacular English. Without all of you, this book would not have been possible.

Finally, thank you to the incredible people who have supported me, cheered me on, shared laughter, encouraged me, and ensured I completed this book. Your positive encouragement and belief in me mean a lot.

I am grateful for this opportunity to spread awareness and share this knowledge with the world. *Thank you!*

About the Author

Franklin R. Jones Jr. is a faculty member at Boston University Wheelock College of Education & Human Development, where he teaches in the Deaf Studies Program. As a Black multigenerational Deaf man, Jones has a personal and professional interest in exploring the history and linguistic and cultural content of Black American Sign Language (BASL). He is also a sought-after speaker on topics related to educational, linguistic, and cultural equity in Deaf communities, with his talks covering a broad range of subjects such as Black Deaf experience, ASL, Deaf culture, linguistics, and pedagogy. His lived experience as a Black Deaf man informs his work and research, and he is dedicated to advancing the field of Deaf studies through his teaching, community engagement, and scholarship.

First published in 2026 by Wellfleet Press, an imprint of The Quarto Group,
142 West 36th Street, 4th Floor, New York, NY 10018, USA
(212) 779-4972 www.Quarto.com

EEA Representation, WTS Tax d.o.o.,
Žanova ulica 3, 4000 Kranj, Slovenia.
www.wts-tax.si

Wellfleet titles are also available at discount for retail, wholesale, promotional, and bulk purchase.
For details, contact the Special Sales Manager by email at specialsales@quarto.com or by mail at
The Quarto Group, Attn: Special Sales Manager, 100 Cummings Center Suite 265D, Beverly, MA 01915 USA.

10 9 8 7 6 5 4 3 2 1

ISBN: 978-1-57715-452-5

Digital edition published in 2026
eISBN: 978-0-7603-9151-8

Library of Congress Cataloging-in-Publication Data

Names: Jones, Franklin R., Jr. author
Title: Learn Black American sign language : a history and complete
  beginner's guide with over 200 words and phrases / Franklin R. Jones Jr.
Description: New York : Wellfleet Press, 2026. | Includes bibliographical
  references and index. | Summary: "Learn Black American Sign Language
  shares details of its history and teaches everyday words alongside
  proper positions and motions of the language with photos and
  descriptions"—Provided by publisher.
Identifiers: LCCN 2025023139 (print) | LCCN 2025023140 (ebook) | ISBN
  9781577154525 | ISBN 9780760391518 ebook
Subjects: LCSH: American Sign Language--Usage | African
  Americans—Communication | Black people--United States--Communication |
  Deaf culture—United States
Classification: LCC HV2476.4 .J66 2026 (print) | LCC HV2476.4 (ebook) |
  DDC 419/.7—dc23/eng/20250806
LC record available at https://lccn.loc.gov/2025023139
LC ebook record available at https://lccn.loc.gov/2025023140

Group Publisher: Rage Kindelsperger
Editorial Director: Erin Canning
Creative Director: Laura Drew
Managing Editor: Cara Donaldson
Editors: Elizabeth You and Katelynn Abraham
Art Direction: Marisa Kwek, Beth Middleworth
Cover Design: Beth Middleworth
Interior Design: Angela Williams
Photography: Nick Nogueira, except where noted; Bridgeman Images: 7 (Stanley B. Burns, MD
& The Burns Archive), 10 (Everett Collection, Inc.); Getty Images: 183 (Valerie Macon), 184 (Rob Carr),
185 (Stephen Dunn)
Models: Franklin R. Jones Jr. and Stephanie Hakulin

Printed in Huizhou, Guangdong, China TT102025